A SAILMATE BOOK

USING VHF RADIO

—— Brian Faulkner ——

ADLARD COLES NAUTICAL

London

First edition 1992
Published by Adlard Coles Nautical
an imprint of A & C Black (Publishers) Ltd
35 Bedford Row, London WC1R 4JH

ISBN 0-7136-3610-6

A CIP catalogue record for this book is available
from the British Library.

Typeset in 11/12pt Century
Printed and bound in Great Britain by
J. W. Arrowsmith Ltd., Bristol BS3 2NT

Contents

Acknowledgements

I would like to acknowledge the help of the following: staff at Lands End Radio and HM Coastguard Falmouth; Penzance Harbourmaster; Seacom Electronics, Newlyn; Icom (UK), Thanet; Lawrence Lawry, Alec Blakely.

Why do I need a VHF radio?

Have you just bought a VHF radio for your boat? Do you already have one fitted or are you thinking of buying one?

With more and more people buying boats for leisure purposes, a VHF radio is becoming an increasingly important and indispensable piece of equipment. It is still, however, a mysterious, area in the minds of many boat owners, even those who have passed the relevant R/T exam.

Let me ask you a few more questions. Why did you buy the set? Why are you thinking of buying a set? Is there really a need to have one?

Perhaps the last question is the most pertinent. Why have one at all? Most people, when asked, will reply that there is a need. If pressed further, they will say that it's nice to know that if they get into trouble they can shout for help, knowing that there are professionals listening.

Is that the only reason for having a VHF radio? If it is, then it would seem to be an expensive luxury based on the assumption that the number of times you will have to call for help will, hopefully, be minimal. For most small boat owners, a plentiful supply of flares would be cheaper.

Some people install sets to make the occasional phone call home to tell the family that they will be late back. That's fair

1

enough but again it's an expensive luxury. There are also people, of course, who have to buy any new gadget that comes on the market whether or not it is of use to them. After the initial enthusiasm wears off it is hardly used and is relegated to the shelf, often to be sold later at a knockdown price.

Are you one of those boat owners who only switches your VHF on when you actually want to use it? There seems little point in spending several hundred pounds for a piece of equipment which will not be used to its full capability.

'Right!' I hear you say, 'If you're so clever how should we use our set?'

Well, a VHF radio is probably one of the most important and useful pieces of equipment that a boat owner can have; on a par with compass, flares and lifejackets. It is not only a means of establishing contact with the shore in case of an emergency or to make the odd phone call, it is an excellent information medium; a complete communication system in fact.

Without doing anything apart from switching on the set, you can hear the vast amount of information that is broadcast throughout the day by all types of radio stations. If you do no more than switch on the set when you weigh anchor and switch off when you tie up at the end of the day you will have had a complete picture of what has been happening around you, purely by listening.

What will you hear?

First, you will receive full details of any distress in your area and through this you may find that you're in a position to help a fellow mariner. How would you feel if you arrived home, switched on the TV news and found that the fellow you thought was waving at you was, in fact, requiring assistance? It has happened.

Weather forecasts and gale warnings are broadcast by Coast Radio Stations and HM Coastguard who, in addition, issue small craft wind warnings and forecasts for inshore waters. Coast Stations issue warnings of navigational hazards and broadcast regular traffic lists - lists of vessels they have telephone calls for.

All this information should be of interest, and is available without you having to do anything other than switch on your set and occasionally change to a working channel.

If all this is available without doing very much, what is available with a little more effort? The obvious thing, apart from emergency communications, is the ship to shore telephone service through Coast Radio Stations, which enables you to make calls to and from the shore. Coast Stations can also provide free medical advice by connecting you to a doctor. HM Coastguard will accept position reports from you and will give local weather forecasts on request. You will also be in contact with other boats near you and will be able to advise marinas direct of your imminent arrival.

Some lighthouses are fitted with radio beacons which can be used in conjunction with VHF radios to give bearings, although these are now being phased out. HM Coastguard have VHF direction finders which lock on to transmissions from a boat's VHF – a very useful device in the event of an emergency, especially in fog.

Have I convinced you there is more to VHF radio than meets the eye? No? Well perhaps you might make up your mind after you've read this true story.

A yacht with two people on board left a small harbour on the south coast for a trip that should have taken around six hours. The boat never arrived at its destination, and a friend who was meeting the vessel became worried when 24 hours later it still had not turned up. He reported his worries to the Coastguard who, along with Coast Radio Stations, put out broadcasts to shipping asking them to look out for the yacht. A Nimrod reconnaissance aircraft, two helicopters and two life-boats spent many hours searching over 1800 square miles of sea but there were no sightings. Then, two days later, the yacht sailed into port completely unaware of what was going on. The reason? *The boat had no radio.*

The weather had been good so the crew had decided to carry on sailing, thinking that their companion ashore would not be too worried. If they had carried a radio they could have contacted their friend to tell him of their change of plan. The result? A lot of time and money wasted and a good deal of anguish for those ashore waiting for news.

Convinced now? Then read on!

What is VHF radio?

Is there any need for you to know how a marine radio works? The simple answer is no. You probably have radio or television sets at home but you won't know what happens inside them. However, a brief run through the basics of VHF should help you appreciate just what your equipment is capable of, along with its limitations. It will also enable you to answer questions in the VHF exam with confidence.

What does VHF stand for?

It is simply the abbreviation for Very High Frequency. The radio frequency band is divided into sections ranging from Very Low Frequency (VLF) through Medium and High Frequency (MF and HF) to Super High Frequency (SHF) and above.

VHF is the portion of the radio band from 30 to 300 Megahertz. One Hertz is one cycle of radiation per second so 30 Megahertz is 30 million cycles per second. Only a very small portion of this band, from 156.00 to 162.00 Megahertz, is

What is VHF radio?

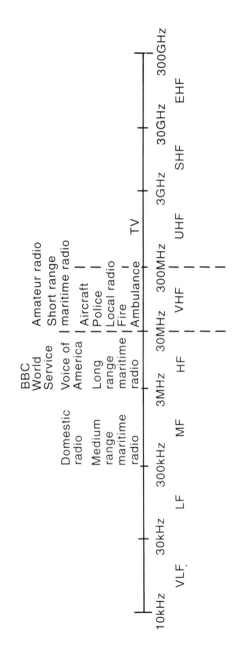

Fig 1 Frequency spectrum

allocated to the maritime user. The rest is divided between such bodies as fire, police, ambulance, aircraft and local radio. Figure 1 shows how the frequency spectrum is made up.

Channels

The marine portion is further subdivided into channels each 25 kilohertz wide, one kilohertz being one thousand hertz. There are 55 of these channels available, each of which has a designated number and a specific use.

Originally there were only 28 channels, each 50 kilohertz apart, Channel 01 to Channel 28. In the early 1970s there was a great upsurge in the use of VHF which resulted in much congestion of these 28 channels. More were obviously needed but the limits of the marine band could not be extended. Instead it was decided to reduce the width of each channel from 50kHz to 25kHz, thereby reducing the gap between channels to 25kHz. This allowed extra channels, known as interleaved channels, designated 60 to 88 to be created. Why, you may ask, are they not labelled Channels 29 to 55. A good point. These channel numbers had already been allocated as Private Channels, which we will talk about later, so a compromise had to be made.

Table 1 (pages 12–13) shows all the channel numbers and their uses. As you can see, some are used exclusively by one type of user whilst others are shared. You will also see that some channels have single frequency while others have two.

Simplex and Duplex

Single frequency channels are called Simplex; the others are called Duplex. Most communications that you will make will use Simplex which, as its name implies, is simple. Basically the

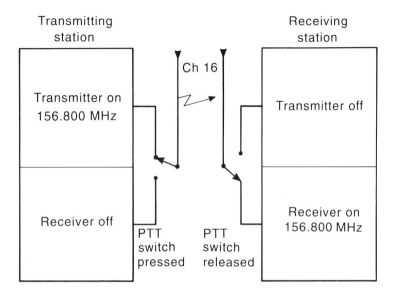

Fig 2 Simplex operation

transmitter and receiver use the same frequency and the same aerial, so with this method of working you cannot talk and listen at the same time. Figure 2 illustrates this.

When you transmit, a relay inside the set switches off the receiver so that even if the other party speaks while you are talking, you won't be able to hear him, nor will he be able to hear you. In the Simplex mode the press to talk (PTT) switch on the side of the handset or microphone must be pressed when you are speaking. This activates the relay which switches off the receiver. After you have finished speaking you must say OVER and release the switch. This indicates to the other person that you have finished and he can speak.

Duplex, on the other hand, in its full form allows for normal conversation to take place, such as you would have when making a telephone call at home. It is, however, only used when making telephone calls through a Coast Radio Station. Unlike Simplex, where both parties transmit and receive on the same frequency using the same aerial, Duplex makes use of two frequencies, one for the shore party and the other for the boat. These frequencies should be as far apart as possible to avoid any chance of breakthrough from one to the other. Looking at the frequencies in Table 1 (pages 12–13) you can see that this is in fact the case. Channel 27, for instance, has a ship frequency of 157.350MHz while the shore frequency is 161.950MHz. Figure 3 shows how Duplex works.

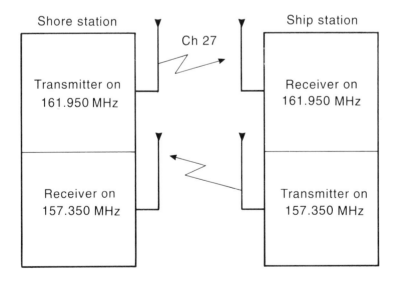

Fig 3 Duplex operation

At the beginning of this section I said that Duplex in its full form allowed for normal two way conversation to take place. Full Duplex requires two aerials, one for transmitting, the other for receiving, and it is here that the small boat owner has a problem. The aerials should be as far apart as possible to reduce the likelihood of interference, but on a yacht or motor cruiser there is very little room to do this. Fortunately it is possible to use one aerial; this system is known as Semi Duplex. The person ashore can talk and listen simultaneously but the boat owner has to use the set in the Simplex mode.

Range

Another question often asked is: What is the range of my radio? This is not as easy to answer as you might suppose because it depends on a great number of variables. In theory, the range of VHF is limited to line of sight, as radio waves at this frequency do not bend around the curvature of the earth. However, under certain atmospheric conditions, normally associated with high pressure and very hot weather, distances of several hundred miles have been achieved. I once talked from a ship in the Indian Ocean to another in the Persian Gulf using VHF, but this is the exception to the rule.

Generally the height of the aerial above sea level at each station is the most important factor in determining range, as the higher the aerial the longer the range. To give you some idea, assuming they are transmitting on full power, two yachts with aerials around 30 feet above sea level would have a range in the order of 15 miles. Communication with a Coast Radio Station, whose aerials might be several hundred feet above sea level should be possible up to about 35 miles. Ranges of handheld sets using their own rubber aerials would be around 15 miles ship to ship and half as much again with a Coast Radio Station. Figure 4 illustrates the principles of VHF propagation and range for various types of craft and equipment.

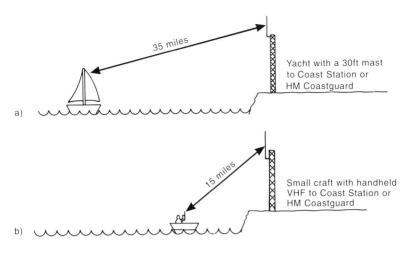

a) Yacht with a 30ft mast to Coast Station or HM Coastguard — 35 miles

b) Small craft with handheld VHF to Coast Station or HM Coastguard — 15 miles

c) Two yachts with 30ft masts — 15 miles

Two dinghies with handheld VHF — 5 miles

e) Yacht with 30ft mast to dinghy with handheld VHF — 10 miles

Fig 4 **VHF typical ranges**

TABLE 1: INTERNATIONAL VHF CHANNELS

Channel no		Ship station frequency	Shore station frequency	Function of channel
00		156.000	156.000	HM Coastguard – *Private*
	60	156.025	160.625	
01		156.050	160.650	
	61	156.075	160.675	
02		156.100	160.700	
	62	156.125	160.725	Public correspondence &
03		156.150	160.750	Port operations
	63	156.175	160.775	
04		156.200	160.800	
	64	156.225	160.825	
05		156.250	160.850	
	65	156.275	160.875	
06		156.300		Intership *only*
	66	156.325	160.925	Public correspondence &
07		156.350	160.950	Port operations
	67	156.375	156.375	Small boat safety (British)
08		156.400		Intership *only*
	68	156.425	156.425	Port operations *only*
09		156.450	156.450	
	69	156.475	156.475	Intership & Port operations
10		156.500	156.500	
	70	156.525	156.525	**Digital Selective Calling for Distress & Safety**
11		156.550	156.550	
	71	156.575	156.575	Port operations *only*
12		156.600	156.600	
	72	156.625		Intership *only*
13		156.650	156.650	
	73	156.675	156.675	Intership & Port operations
14		156.700	156.700	
	74	156.725	156.725	Port operations *only*
15		156.750	156.750	Intership & Port operations

TABLE 1 Cont.

Channel no	Ship station frequency	Shore station frequency	Function of channel
75	Guard Band 156.7625–156.7875MHz		
16	156.800	156.800	**Distress, Safety & Calling**
76	Guard Band 156.8125–156.8375MHz		
17	156.850	156.850	Intership & Port operations
77	156.875		Intership *only*
18	156.900	161.500	Port operations *only*
78	156.925	161.525	Public correspondence & Port operations
19	156.950	161.550	
79	156.975	161.575	
20	157.000	161.600	Port operations *only*
80	157.025	161.625	
21	157.050	161.650	
81	157.075	161.675	Public correspondence & Port operations
22	157.100	161.700	Port operations only
82	157.125	161.725	Public correspondence & Port operations
23	157.150	161.750	
83	157.175	161.775	Public corrrespondence *only*
24	157.200	161.800	
84	157.225	161.825	Public correspondence & Port operations
25	157.250	161.850	
85	157.275	161.875	
26	157.300	161.900	
86	157.325	161.925	Public correspondence
27	157.350	161.950	
87	157.375	161.975	
28	157.400	162.000	
88	157.425	162.025	

Transmitter power

Some owners believe that they can increase the range of their set by increasing the output power of the transmitter. This is an incorrect assumption; power is not important with VHF. Doubling your power from 5 to 10 watts, for instance, will not give you double the range. It is power radiated at the aerial which is important and which is why your aerial must be the best you can afford and be correctly mounted and connected to the set.

The maximum power allowed for a VHF transmitter installed on a boat is 25 watts, with handheld sets being limited to 5 watts.

When using a VHF set minimum transmitting power should be used whenever possible because this results in less interference with other stations. All sets have a low power switch to reduce the output to around 1 watt and low power should always be used when the station you are talking to is fairly close; in harbours and marinas and ship to ship, for example. However, high or full power should always be used when talking to a Coast Radio Station or HM Coastguard. By putting out the strongest signal possible, there will be no danger of the Coastguard not hearing you and will ensure that Coast Radio Station equipment operates correctly, especially if your boat is rolling or pitching or you are operating towards the maximum of your range.

Capture effect

VHF makes use of a phenomenon known as capture effect. If you listen on domestic radio on medium wave especially at night, a great number of signals can be received at the same time on the same frequency. This makes it very difficult to hear the station you actually want. VHF does not suffer from this problem. Because of the method of producing the signal at these

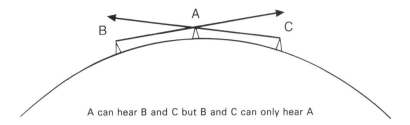

A can hear B and C but B and C can only hear A

Fig 5 Capture effect

frequencies, receivers can only receive one signal at a time, so it follows that the strongest will be produced at the loudspeaker to the exclusion of all others.

Figure 5 shows the principle of capture effect. Station B can hear both station A and station C, while A and C are only able to talk to B, not to each other.

That, then, is the basic concept of VHF. We can now move on to the selection and fitting of the equipment itself.

What type of radio should I buy?

Hopefully you are now convinced that you really do need a VHF radio. What sort should you buy?

Look in any chandler or boat magazine and you'll see a wide range of equipment with an equally wide price range. First list your priorities. For instance, do you need a set that scans through the channels? Do you need a set that has memories or one with Selcall? Do you need an external speaker or a telephone handset? There are lots of so called features on modern VHF sets which the average boat owner would never use.

Until a few years ago, equipment was crystal controlled, which meant that you needed a different crystal for each channel used. Sets would only have space for a certain number of crystals, so it was necessary to know exactly which channels you intended to use. Today all sets are synthesised. That means they can transmit and receive on all 55 international channels, so the problems associated with the old sets are no longer with us. All sets, apart from handheld, now have a maximum transmitter output power of 25W with a switch to reduce this to 1W for use when working stations close to you.

When you obtain a pile of leaflets from a chandler on VHFs it can be quite daunting to see all the fabulous features on offer.

Many of the terms used will not be understandable and the whole process can become totally confusing. Let's find a way through this maze.

Technical data

For a start you can ignore all the technical data listed for the transmitter and receiver, it is almost the same for every piece of equipment on the market. The fact that the sensitivity of the receiver is less than $0.3\mu V$ for 12dB SINAD may mean something to some of you, or the fact that the audio frequency response of the transmitter is $+1$, $-3db$ of 6db/octave pre-emphasis characteristic from 300 to 3000Hz with a 1000Hz reference!

The general specifications given will show the size of the set, which might be important if you've only a small space; they do differ quite considerably in their size. They will all say that they meet MPT 1251 specification, as must all sets before they can be put on the market. Some quote MPT 1252 as well. This is a commercial specification designed to meet the more stringent demands of larger vessels such as fishing boats.

Once we've cleared the chaff we are left with the wonderful features that each manufacturer is trying to tempt you with. Let's go through these features and see what they mean. Hopefully by the end of the list you will have a better idea of what you really need in a set.

As we have already mentioned, all new VHFs are capable of transmitting and receiving on all 55 international channels.

Private channels

Private channels are for use by users authorised by the Department of Trade for private use. They are normally given to such

A selection of typical VHF equipment showing three examples of sets with fist mikes and one with a telephone handset. At the back are two handheld sets with rubber aerials which can be unplugged to allow the boat's main aerial to be attached.

bodies as ferry companies, salvage companies and firms who need the use of a VHF channel for long periods. Obviously they cannot be allowed to congest normal channels so they are granted a private channel for their exclusive use. Boat owners are allocated one too, Channel M (Channel 37), already installed on most sets. The necessary authority to operate on this channel normally comes with your licence. Channel Zero is another which has been issued for use by HM Coastguard for communicating with lifeboats and helicopters.

It is highly unlikely that a small boat owner would be allowed a private channel of his own.

Channel memory

Some sets have the facility to store the most often-used channels in a memory, which then requires only a single push of a button to bring it on line. The number of memory channels varies from five to ten depending on the set. You might consider that it is not really necessary to have this facility when you only have to turn a knob or press a keypad to bring the channels up anyway. Batteries keep the information stored when the set is switched off.

Dual watch

This is quite a useful facility which most sets have. You can monitor Channel 16 while another channel is scanned at the same time. If a signal comes up on this channel, the set automatically settles on it. You can instantly switch back to Channel 16. Scanning takes place about once every second and you can talk on the selected channel while still keeping a watch on 16.

Channel scanning

On some sets it is possible to scan all channels or just the ones in the memory. As another plus, you can override any of the channels to limit the scanning selection if you like. One problem with scanning is that if a signal comes up on, say, your first channel but the scanning is at another point in its cycle, you can miss the first word of the call or message.

Waterproofing

Some equipment manufacturers go as far as to say their sets are water resistant, others say they are splashproof while the majority say nothing at all. At least one set on the market pronounces that it is waterproof and has been tested to a depth of one metre. If you're going to use a radio at that depth perhaps you should be indulging in diving rather than boating!

Telephone-type handset

Nearly all sets come with a fist mike with the PTT (press to talk) switch built in. Most of these can have a telephone type handset fitted as an optional extra although one or two have it as standard. The advantage of this type of handset is that you are not straining to listen to the loudspeaker of the radio which might be a little distance away. This is especially important if you are likely to make many link calls or if your boat is particularly noisy.

External speaker

All sets have a built in loudspeaker but, as the equipment is most likely to be fitted below decks, it is useful to have a waterproof external speaker so that you can, at least, listen to what is going on without having to go below.

Selcall

I don't imagine that many people will need this facility but if you receive many link calls from the shore it might be worth considering. Selective calling is a system whereby a Coast Station can inform you that a link call has been booked without the need for you to listen to traffic lists. Your boat will have a five figure code which is converted into tones at the Coast Station and transmitted on Channel 16. Your receiver then decodes the signal and indicates that a call has been received. On some equipment this brings up a light, on others the four figure identification of the station calling.

Channel display

Most sets, nowadays, have a digital read-out showing the number of the channel that you have selected. One or two have thumbwheel switches to select the channel or knobs with the numbers etched in plastic around the edge. Digital displays will show you whether you are in Simplex or Duplex mode and will indicate when the transmitter is working. Other models will have one LED which is lit when the transmitter is on and another to show you are in Simplex.

Power

Most sets work off your boat's 12V supply but DC-DC converters, which convert 24V to 12V, can be bought. Some equipment will also work with a rectifier from 110 or 220V AC mains.

Knobs and switches

The trend today is to choose touch switches for items such as channel selection or selecting power output, especially if the set has a memory. Some use push buttons for these functions, but all use old fashioned switches for on/off, gain and squelch control. Your choice will obviously be a personal one.

Handheld VHF

So far we have talked about the bulkhead or console mounted VHF, but you might want the advantage of being able to use your set in a dinghy.

Modern handheld sets can perform all the functions of a fixed set although if you are using its own helical aerial the range will be significantly less. This can be overcome by buying an adapter so that you can fit a normal VHF aerial to it. Again we'll go through the facilities available on this type of set.

Most are capable of working on all 55 international channels, some using thumbwheel switches, in which case the controls are on the top of the equipment; some with push buttons and digital channel readout where the controls will be on the front. On all models the PTT switch will be on the side with some form of indication that you are transmitting; either an LED or a message on the digital readout.

Some models have Channel 16 and 6 fitted as standard and up to ten spot frequencies. Some have the ability to store up to ten channels with a battery backup to keep the memory alive when the set is switched off. Volume and squelch controls are usually of the knob variety. The more expensive models have scanning and dual watch facilities.

Most have an external speaker/microphone socket and have provision for a DC supply instead of its own internal NICAD batteries. Lapel microphones and rapid battery chargers are also available. These sets come in a package with batteries, battery charger, carrying case and strap.

A good operating position for a handheld set. Notice how the aerial is upright and not angled to one side, ensuring good transmission of signals.

Considering that they are designed to be carried around in dinghies and the like, very few are said to be water resistant. It is possible to get either a rigid waterproof case or a flexible one which looks like a big plastic food bag. Both types allow you to use the set while it is in the bag.

Secondhand equipment

What happens if you buy a secondhand boat with a radio already fitted? Most secondhand boats will have the type of VHF described above, but it is still possible that you might buy one which has the old type crystal controlled model. In this case you will have to make sure that you can still obtain crystals for it and plan your channels carefully, taking into account whether you will be making many link calls, using the marina channel or talking intership. These sets will come with Channel 16 and Channel 6 fitted, which is mandatory, but you might be limited to eight or ten other channels. Channels 8 and 10 for intership, 12 and 14 for harbours, the marina channel and 67 for HM Coastguard will probably be the only others you need. If you want to make link calls you will have to decide which stations you are most likely to use and get crystals for the appropriate channels. Your local marine radio dealer will be able to help you.

Squelch

All VHF radios have a knob marked Squelch, but what is it and what does it do?

Squelch controls the sensitivity of the receiver. If you turn the control to minimum you will hear the familiar roaring noise from the speaker. This noise is generated from within the set itself and when you receive a signal it disappears. You should set your squelch control to the point where the noise just disappears. This is known as the squelch threshold. The only problem is that on days when propagation is good, signals which are really outside your range and too weak to understand are received. Turning up the squelch control means that only strong local signals are heard.

Aerials

There are a large number of different aerials on the market but they are all variations of the stainless steel whip, glass fibre whip or, if you have a handheld, a helical. All types work equally well. The glass fibre whip has low windage so would be ideal if you have a fast boat. It will bend, but you shouldn't experience any deterioration in transmission or reception. Low loss cable normally comes with the aerial and in most cases will be long enough to run from the top of a mast to the back of the set without having to make a join. In fact joining aerial cable should be avoided as each joint introduces considerable losses into the system and therefore reduces the efficiency of the equipment. If it is unavoidable, make sure that you use the same type of low loss cable and make a proper plug and socket joint. Your local dealer will be able to help you with this.

Let's assume that you have dipped into your pocket and are now the proud owner of a VHF transceiver.

Installation

Your next problem is how to install the equipment correctly. Obviously you can get someone to do it for you; the firm you bought it from will probably do it. If you ask a friend of a friend to do it for you, make sure he really knows what he is doing. If you are fairly handy and can fit a radio in a car you should have little difficulty doing the work yourself. Let's start from the top and work down.

Fitting the aerial

We have already said that the aerial is possibly the most important item, so it *must* be fitted correctly. Make sure that it is as high as possible and securely attached to the mast or cabin; waterproof deck glands and O-rings must be used wherever a cable passes through a bulkhead. Securely fix the cable coming down the mast so that it doesn't flap around; solder the plug to the lead. Figure 6 shows the correct way to do this.

It is not only the small boat owner who has problems with VHF aerials – even the professional can suffer. I was once on a ship carrying cars from Japan to Central America and the Red Sea. At nearly every port, the Captain called me at ungodly hours because he could not contact pilots or agents. Despite having the set and aerials checked by shore technicians on two different occasions, the problem persisted, so while at anchor at

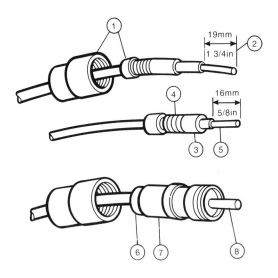

1. Feed coupling nut and reducing adaptor over cable.
2. Cut back outer sheath 19mm (1 3/4in).
3. Position reducing adaptor flush with end of sheath.
4. Fold back braid over reducing adaptor. Trim off just before threaded portion.
5. Cut back inner insulation 16mm (5/8in).
6. Holding cable and reducing adaptor, screw body assembly tightly home. The inner conductor should be flush with end of plug.
7. Solder braid to body through holes (a large soldering iron will be needed around 60W).
8. Solder inner conductor to plug end and screw coupling nut over body.

Fig 6 Fitting an aerial plug

a suitable port and with the ship swinging I carried out some tests on the set myself. Sure enough in certain positions the shore station could not hear me. By plotting the positions on a chart I discovered that there was a blind spot when the ship was in a certain position and, on investigation, I found that part of a mast was between the transmitting aerial and the shore when this occurred. Resiting the aerial solved the problem.

Siting the set

Siting the set itself is a major decision. The most important thing to remember is to keep it well away from spray and away from anything that might fall on it or cause other damage. Do not fit it where it will be in direct sunlight; make sure that there is a free flow of air around it. Do not site it within 18 in (46cm) of the boat's compass or it could cause problems.

Make sure that all external connections, aerial, speaker (especially the earth) are securely made to a good bonding point.

Wherever possible, connect the power leads straight to the battery through an isolating switch. The red wire (positive) connects to the + terminal and the black (negative) to the − terminal. If you need to extend the leads make sure you use the same type of cable. Use a proper junction box (don't wrap the wires together and cover with a piece of insulating tape) and make the extension as short as possible. A fuse holder and fuse should come with the set.

Sets today come in various sizes; some will fit on to the bulkhead, some on the deckhead and some in a console. They all come with mounting brackets which are easily secured with a few screws.

If you are fitting an extension speaker outside, make sure that the wiring is tidy and the cable passes through waterproof glands where it passes through a bulkhead or into the speaker itself. Figure 7 shows in block diagram form the installation process. Right we're nearly there. You have bought your set and have installed it.

What type of radio should I buy?

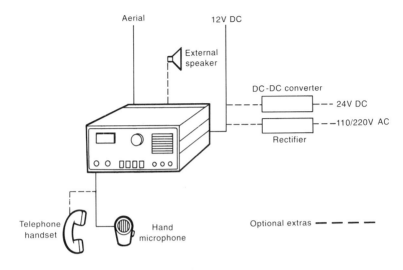

Fig 7 Block diagram of a typical VHF installation

Licences

Do you have a licence? Two licences are required before you can operate your new VHF; one for you, the operator, and the other for the equipment.

Authority to operate
The operator's licence is also called the certificate of competence or authority to operate. This is the same as having a driving licence for a car, and once you have passed the exam the licence is yours for life. In the UK, the Royal Yachting Association organises the exam, and provided you use a bit of common sense, you should have little difficulty in passing. Your local yacht club or the RYA will be able to tell you where and when the next course is to take place. Booklets G22 and G26 are available from the RYA and are useful guides to what you will need to know to pass the exam.

The minimum age for taking the exam is 16. The 'Authority to Operate' on British vessels is normally only granted to British subjects, although foreigners who live in the UK permanently and who own a vessel flying the Red Ensign can be granted an Authority to Operate on their own named vessel if they apply to the Department of Transport.

We are only interested here in the VHF exam which gives you the 'Restricted Certificate of Competence in Radio Telephony (VHF only)'. In addition to giving you the authority to operate, it also carries a declaration that you will not divulge any information that you might hear while listening. The exam itself consists of a written part followed by a practical on VHF procedures during which you will have to show the examiner that you can use a VHF set correctly.

Equipment licence

The equipment licence is on the same basis as a television licence or car tax and is renewable each year. It authorises you to have two way communication with other vessels and Coast Stations. An application form is usually supplied when you buy your equipment but if you are in doubt, contact the Radio Communication Division of the Department of Trade and Industry at the address in Appendix H.

There are conditions attached to the licence. One of these states that the set must only be operated under the control of someone holding the appropriate certificate of competence. Other conditions include maximum power output and frequencies that can be used.

When you receive the licence it will show your boat's name and the callsign that has been allocated as well as something called your Public Correspondence category. This simply indicates the hours of watch you keep for sending and receiving private messages. In the case of a small craft this will be HX, which means these times are irregular. Passenger ships are H24, having a radio watch throughout the day and night, while cargo ships are normally H8, having a watch for 8 hours of the day.

If you change your boat, the callsign remains with it. You will either receive a new one when you install a set on your next boat or, if a set is already fitted, you will inherit the existing one. Don't forget to make sure your radio bill is paid up to date when you sell a boat or the new owner will receive your bills.

Receive only

If you decide that you would never want to make use of a full transceiver but might want to monitor certain broadcasts, you can obtain a Receive Only licence. This authorises you to listen to port operations frequencies, radio beacons and broadcasts from Coast Stations such as weather forecasts which are intended for general reception.

The Radio Communication Division of the DTI issues a free booklet called Licensing of Radio Telephone Apparatus which can be obtained from them at the address in Appendix H.

Documents

As well as your Authority to Operate and the vessel's equipment licence you should have a copy of Section 11 of the Post Office (Protection) Act 1884 which covers the secrecy of communications and which comes with your licence. You also need to have a list of Coast Stations covering the stations that you are likely to communicate with. This could be the *Admiralty List of Radio Signals* volume 1 part 1, or one of the yachtsman's almanacs which give this information.

Radio-telephone log

It is not compulsory for you to carry a radio-telephone log, but in the event of a distress you must make a note of the various messages you receive or make. If you decide to keep a log it must include:

- The operator's name and the dates and times that the equipment was switched on and off.
- Time of arriving and leaving port.
- A summary of all distress, safety and urgency working.
- A record of your working with the shore (link calls etc) and other vessels.
- A note of any major failure such as power or equipment.
- The position of the vessel at least once a day.

Radio frequency interference (RFI)

This can be a major problem. Interference is generated by a varying or interrupted current flow in cables and wires. You've probably heard it on car radios when the windscreen wipers are switched on and a buzzing sound comes out of the speakers. It should not be too much of a problem in modern boats; interference will have been taken into account when the craft was built. Older vessels, which have had electronic equipment added, can present more of a problem. If you are in any doubt as to what to do there are companies that specialise in RFI problems.

Causes of RFI

Ignition circuits, rotating propellor shafts, wiring, even fluorescent lights can be culprits. In some severe cases, even the boat's railings have been found to be the cause. It can travel through the boat's wiring or superstructure; if you have a great deal of wiring bunched together, the cables carrying the interference can radiate it to other cables causing even more of a problem.

How can you get rid of this apparent nightmare? As was stated earlier it should not be too much of a problem in modern boats, but curing it depends on the type of interference you have and where it is coming from.

The only sure way of discovering where it is coming from is to switch off equipment and see what happens to the noise.

31

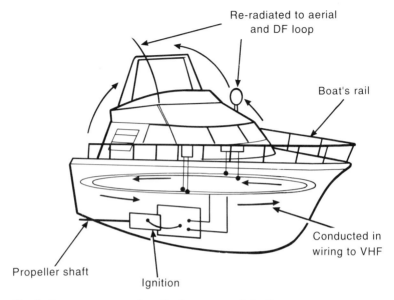

Fig 8 Some causes of radio frequency interference

If it disappears, the equipment you have just switched off is causing it; if it remains, it must be due to something else. Once you have found the cause then a combination of screening, shielding or filtering should help as detailed below.

If you have a petrol engine, the problem may lie in the ignition. Check to see if the problem is the engine itself or the alternator or dynamo. Stop the engine, disconnect the alternator and see if the noise disappears when you start up again; then do the same with the dynamo. If you find that the interference is caused by the engine itself, try repositioning the ignition coil; bonding it to the engine block and fitting an anti-suppression capacitor between the low tension wire and earth. Try to make all leads as short as possible and use anti-suppression leads to the plugs.

Interference from the alternator or dynamo can be reduced by using screened cable and by keeping cable runs as short as possible. Sheathed cable should have its outer braid connected to a common earth. Replacing the brushes and cleaning the

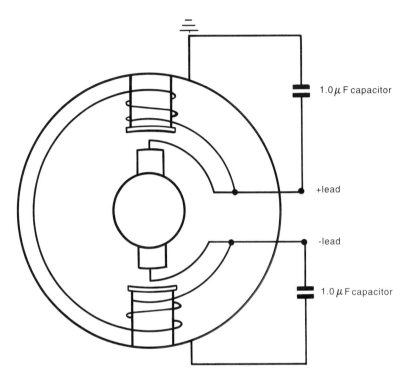

Fig 9 Connecting anti-suppression capacitors

commutator might help, or perhaps fitting a large anti-suppression capacitor may solve the problem.

Other motors, such as bilge pumps, can cause interference and, again, fitting capacitors between power leads and earth should help. Try to keep wiring looms as small as possible and route cables different ways so that the chance of transferring interference from cable to cable is reduced. If possible, keep cables carrying power away from other cables.

As far as your radio and any other electronic equipment is concerned the watchword is, 'good earths'. Make sure they are all well earthed.

Using your set

Once you have passed your VHF exam and have installed a VHF on your boat, what comes next? Using your radio might seem to be an easy matter but it's rather like taking a driving test; once you've passed the exam you really start to learn. It's all very well sitting in a yacht club or classroom doing everything 'by the book'; in the real world things have a habit of not exactly following the rules. A few words of advice will not go amiss and will give you that extra confidence when working with professional operators such as Coastguards for the first time.

The most important rule to remember when using your VHF is to always *listen first before calling* to ensure that the channel is free for your use.

Voice technique

People tend to be self conscious when going on the air for the first time, which is perfectly natural. Radio is a very impersonal medium; you cannot see the person you are talking to, you don't know him and you probably don't really know where he is.

The first thing to remember is to try to speak naturally, as if you were having a telephone call with a friend down the road. If you listen to professional operators, you'll notice that they speak in a normal voice. Some books on the subject suggest you speak at a slightly higher pitch than normal, but this can make you sound even more unnatural. You may find it easier to have someone standing next to you when you are speaking; talk to them as if they are the person you are trying to contact.

The problem of being self conscious can work the other way as well. I once saw a group of local radio presenters at a fête, terrified of talking to a crowd because they could actually see them!

Keep the microphone about six inches away from your mouth and don't shout; you've spent a lot of money on equipment that will amplify your voice for you. Plan what you want to say in advance and, if necessary, write it down; it will stop you drying up or waffling.

Phonetics

A good tip is to have the name and callsign of your boat written out phonetically by the radio so that you can read it off without having a lot of 'ers' and 'ahs' while you think of the correct phonetic word. It sounds much more professional. Many's the time that a Coast Station operator, faced with a yachtsman trying frantically to remember the callsign of his boat and then associate that with the phonetic alphabet, has put him out of his misery. '*Nonsuch*, try Two Alpha Bravo Charlie.'

It's not the end of the world if you can't remember the correct phonetic letter; use any word that begins with that letter, so long as it isn't rude. The operator at the other end might make a few uncomplimentary comments about 'Yachties' to his colleagues but you won't hear them and you'll still get the message across which is the main thing. The phonetic alphabet is given in Appendix A. One point to note: if you're transmitting figures, each digit is sent separately.

65 is spoken as six five and not sixty five.

3250 is spoken as three two five zero.

0 is always spoken as zero, never nought.

Typical deckhead mounted VHF. The telephone handset is kept in the bracket to the left of the set. By unscrewing the nuts on either side of the mounting, the set can be removed for security.

Once you have taken the plunge and called someone, the next hurdle is getting an answer and then knowing what to say next. The rest of this chapter is designed to give you a good idea of how to call various types of station and the sort of things you will be saying to them.

Control of communication

If you are in contact with HM Coastguard or a Coast Station, it is the shore station that controls communication. The only exception to this is when there is distress, safety or urgency work going on. If you are talking ship to ship, it is the vessel that has been called that has control. The reason for this is that when you call another boat, you don't know if it is convenient for him to talk at that time. He may, for instance, be already talking to another station which is out of your range, in which case your call to him will cause interference. He would acknowledge your call, finish working with the other station and call you back.

HM Coastguard

Let's take the Coastguard first as these are the people you are most likely to be in contact with. HM Coastguard is responsible for co-ordinating Search and Rescue operations around the coast of the United Kingdom and 1000 miles out into the North Atlantic. When they are dealing with an emergency they can call on RNLI lifeboats, Royal Navy and Royal Air Force helicopters, merchant and naval ships, Royal Air Force fixed wing aircraft such as the Nimrod; in fact anyone who may be able to give assistance. They have their own fleet of inflatables for inshore emergencies and at Lee-on-Solent, Sumburgh and Stornoway they have Search and Rescue helicopters. The Channel Navigation Service and the Marine Pollution Control Unit are also operated by the Coastguard.

For Coastguard purposes the coast is divided into six regions, each with a Maritime Rescue Control Centre (MRCC). Each region is further sub-divided into Districts with a Maritime Rescue Sub-Centre (MRSC). Auxiliary Coastguard stations are found in the Districts under the command of a Sector Officer. These stations have rescue vehicles and equipment and can be manned at short notice should an incident occur. Coastguard stations, vehicles and boats are fitted with VHF Channels 0, 6, 10, 16, 67, and 73. MRCCs have direct telephone links with their local Coast Radio Station.

A general view of Falmouth Coastguard operations room. The map on the back wall shows the area covered by Falmouth.

Yacht and Small Boat Safety Scheme

The Coastguard can help the small boat owner in a number of ways. The Yacht and Small Boat Safety Scheme gives your local MRCC information about your boat, its equipment, details of where you normally sail and anything else which might be of use in an emergency such as telephone numbers of shore contacts. You can get the necessary card (CG66) from Coastguard Stations, yacht clubs and marinas. Simply fill it in and post it. If you have a photograph of your boat so much the better, but if you do take advantage of the scheme, which is free, don't forget to update the information if necessary. When you call the Coastguard to give a position report tell him that you have lodged a Form 66. All Coastguard stations have a leaflet on the scheme which they would be only too pleased to let you have.

Channel 16

Channel 16 is the Distress, Safety and Calling channel. Any vessel in distress and using a VHF set to make a MAYDAY call should use Channel 16. In addition, it should be used to make initial contact with another station, prior to moving to a working channel. If possible, a continuous listening watch should be kept on Channel 16 when at sea.

A 24 hour radio watch is kept on Channel 16 around the coast from the MRCCs and MRSCs, and should an incident occur close to the shore Auxiliary Coastguards can be alerted to attend on scene.

Remote VHF radio sites, controlled from the MRCCs and MRSCs, supplement the main stations' equipment and give coverage of virtually the whole of the UK coast. There is no need to know where they are; if you are between Lands End and Falmouth a call to Falmouth Coastguard will solicit a reply using the transmitter closest to you. The operator can tell which is the best one to use. (See the chapter on Distress, Urgency, Medico and Safety.)

Channel 67

The main Coastguard working channel is 67. This channel should be used for traffic which is not urgent enough to be sent on Channel 16. Advising the Coastguard of your position or asking for weather conditions are examples of this type of traffic. Your initial call should be on Channel 16 after which you will be told which channel to go to to continue, normally 67.

A typical non-urgent call to a Coastguard would be as follows:

FALMOUTH COASTGUARD FALMOUTH COASTGUARD FALMOUTH
COASTGUARD
THIS IS YACHT NONSUCH YACHT NONSUCH
POSITION REPORT
OVER

YACHT NONSUCH
THIS IS FALMOUTH COASTGUARD
CHANNEL SIX SEVEN AND STAND BY

THIS IS YACHT NONSUCH
GOING UP

In the example above you will see that the yacht called the Coastguard three times, followed by his name twice. If you went by the book you would transmit both the Coastguard and your boat's name three times, but in practice this would be too long winded and would cause more congestion than is necessary on Channel 16. Once you have moved to a working channel you need only use names once, or not at all as we shall see later.

When the Coastguard gives you a working channel your reply is 'GOING UP'. Some people say 'GOING OVER'. This has caused problems in the past with listeners who haven't taken notice of the previous conversation thinking that a vessel is sinking.

When you move to your working channel, wait for the Coastguard to call you. He may be busy on another channel or listening to someone else; the last thing he wants is you clamouring for attention in the background. Remember it is the shore station that controls communication.

YACHT NONSUCH
THIS IS FALMOUTH COASTGUARD
CHANNEL SIX SEVEN

FALMOUTH COASTGUARD
THIS IS YACHT NONSUCH
I'M JUST LEAVING ST MAWES BOUND PENZANCE,
ETA SIXTEEN HUNDRED
OVER

ROGER NONSUCH
HAVE A GOOD TRIP

THANK YOU FALMOUTH
I'LL BE LISTENING ON CHANNEL SIXTEEN
OUT

You can see again from the above that the use of names becomes less and less until they are hardly used at all. Once you are talking to the Coastguard, you know who he is and he knows who you are, so if you think about it, using names just clutters up the conversation. After all, this is what is happening; it is a conversation between two people who happen to be several miles away from each other.

Looking at the last line of the call you may have noticed that we have broken a rule stated earlier that when you give numbers you should say each one separately. On this occasion the yachtsman says 'Channel 16' and not 'Channel one six'. This is one of those exceptions to the rule. No one really knows why it is acceptable but everyone does it.

There is also an exception to the rule about calling the Coastguard on channel 16. Because of the large number of small craft in the Isle of Wight area during the summer months, Solent Coastguards listen for calls on Channel 67 as well as 16. This keeps a lot of unnecessary traffic off the distress channel. However it is only Solent Coastguard that this applies to. Do not call other Coastguard stations direct on Channel 67 or you will not be popular. Always use Channel 16.

An important point with regard to position/passage reports – *always remember to call in when you reach harbour.* Much Coastguard time and resources have, at times, been wasted on looking for small craft such as fishing or dive boats who announce their expedition and fail to report their safe return.

Channel Zero
HM Coastguard has a private channel on 156.00 MHz, designated Channel Zero. Its use is restricted to HM Coastguard but if you are an auxiliary afloat you might receive permission from the DTI to fit this frequency although it is not automatic. It is normally used by the Coastguard to talk to lifeboats and rescue helicopters.

Channel 70
Channel 70 was an intership channel but has now been set aside for digital selective calling and so must not now be used for communicating by voice. Digital Selective Calling will be in use

in a few years' time by the Coastguard to alert vessels to the fact that a distress call has been received.

Broadcasts
The Coastguard broadcasts weather forecasts, strong wind warnings and local navigational warnings on Channel 67 after an announcement on Channel 16. Weather forecasts are repeated every four hours, or every two if gale warnings or strong wind warnings are in force.

Channel Navigation Information Service
If you are in the Dover Straits, the Dover Coastguard provides a 24 hour Channel Navigation Information Service. Broadcasts are made at forty minutes past the hour on Channel 11 during fine weather, and, in addition, at five minutes to the hour if the weather is poor. The French Coastguard does the same. Information is given on navigational problems, fog and any other troubles which a mariner might encounter in the Dover Strait.

Direction finding
VHF direction finding equipment is sited at strategic points giving coverage of most of Britain's coastal waters. It is primarily for use in emergencies but if you really need it, say in fog, a request to the Coastguard on Channel 16 will produce a bearing with an accuracy of plus or minus two degrees. This is a free service, but don't abuse it by asking for bearings in fine weather.

Safety Traffic
Some people call the Coastguard on Channel 16 saying that they have a safety message. Technically this is incorrect. A safety message, as we shall see later, is a message preceded by the word SAYCUREETAY, normally broadcast by a shore station giving details of navigational warnings. Calling the Coastguard

with a position report for your boat is not Safety traffic in the true sense of the word.

HM Coastguard have various booklets on such subjects as Safety at Sea, and the Channel Navigation Information Service which they will be only too pleased to let you have.

The position of Coastguard stations is shown in Appendix D and visitors are usually welcome. The Station Officer of your nearest MRCC should be able to arrange a visit; don't turn up on the doorstep unannounced.

Coast Radio Stations

Many yachtsmen are under the impression that Coast Radio Stations are part of the Coastguard service. In fact they are operated by British Telecom and staffed in the main by former Merchant Navy Radio Officers. The earliest of these stations was built at the beginning of this century when Marconi was still conducting his experiments into radio.

There are seven manned Coast Stations around the UK coast which remotely control a further 28 stations. If you are within 35 miles of the coast you should have no problem in accessing them. A major reorganisation of Coast Stations has recently taken place and now the country has been split into two regions with four manned stations in the north and three in the south. The two regions are independent of each other and each station within a region can operate the equipment at all the other stations in that region. Appendix E shows the two regions and stations within them.

You would normally be answered by an operator at the station you called, but the system is flexible and if you call Humber Radio and that station is very busy your call could be routed to a station that isn't, for example Niton. The operator at Niton will know that you made your initial call through Humber and will identify himself as Humber Radio.

The Distress Watch position at Lands End Radio showing, in the centre, the VDU and keyboard used for general answering of vessels with (left) the keyboard and screen used for selecting equipment for distress and broadcast working.

Channel 16
Coast Stations do not have an obligation to monitor Channel 16 for distress purposes so only a local watch is kept. It is best not to make any calls to a Coast Station on Channel 16.

Link calls
To make a telephone call to a land number, your home perhaps, all you have to know is which station you are nearest and listen on the appropriate channel. If you hear speech or pips you know that channel is engaged, so you wait until the call has finished or move to another channel. Once you have a clear channel hold

your transmit button down for five or six seconds then release. You should hear pips being radiated. This indicates that you have accessed the system and all you have to do is wait until an operator calls you.

WHO IS CALLING LANDS END RADIO ON CHANNEL 27?

LANDS END RADIO THIS IS TWO ALPHA BRAVO CHARLIE
YACHT NONSUCH ACCOUNTING
AUTHORITY GB14. I'D LIKE A LINK CALL PLEASE.

NONSUCH, LANDS END. THANK YOU
WHAT NUMBER DO YOU WANT?

071 888 1111 PLEASE

OKAY, STANDBY PLEASE

NONSUCH THIS IS LANDS END. GO AHEAD, YOU'RE CONNECTED

Away you go, chatting for as long as you like. If you have a Semi Duplex set you must release the PTT switch each time you have finished speaking or you will not hear what the other person is saying. If you have a full Duplex set, one with an aerial for transmitting and another for receiving, you can make the call talking and listening normally, just as you would at home. Notice the lack of callsigns and names in the exchange above. This is not by the book but is far more practical.

If you do not hear the pips when you make your initial call you are probably out of range of that station. Either try another channel or wait until you are closer. Once the call has finished and the shore party has put the phone down you will hear the pips again. When the operator answers he will know that you are waiting to know the duration of the call (for your billing charge). Wait until he gives you the duration before leaving the channel.

NONSUCH THIS IS LANDS END. THAT WAS FOUR MINUTES

LANDS END THIS IS NONSUCH. THANK YOU. HAVE A GOOD WATCH

The minimum chargeable time is three minutes, with each

subsequent minute charged pro-rata. Unlike your home telephone there are no off peak times, the charges are the same throughout the day.

You will notice that at the beginning of the call the yacht's information was given in a certain order; callsign, name, and accounting authority. This is because the operator is using a computerised system which requires the inputting of information in a particular order.

You may be asked to spell your boat's name, so be prepared for that. It's amazing how many yachts have common names spelt in the most unusual way. There is a point behind this. If the correct spelling is not entered into the computer, any telephone calls booked for you will not be presented to the operator.

Billing

How will you be billed? When you buy your set the dealer should give you a form to enable you to apply for a Ship Licence. One of the questions on this form is, 'Who will settle accounts for R/T calls?' You enter Accounting Indicator Code GB14 (BT's code) here together with an address to which BT can send bills. This shows that you have appointed BT to act as your accounting authority.

Although you have entered GB14 as your accounting authority, the easiest way to have calls billed is by using the YTD system. Yacht Telephone Debit enables you to have the cost of the calls debited to your home telephone number, but it only applies to calls made to the UK. When you give your boat's details to the operator, after stating the accounting authority say: 'I'd like a YTD call please'. He will then ask you for the number you want to be connected to and the number you want the call billed to.

Other calls are debited to your boat's account and you will be sent a bill every quarter. You can also use a British Telecom chargecard details of which can be obtained from your local Telephone Sales office. If you are not told the duration of your call immediately it finishes, don't worry. You will not be charged

Lands End Radio showing a commercial working position. All commercial operations, ranging from the entry of ships' details to operating equipment and dialling telephone numbers, are carried out on keyboards. It is this working point that deals with MEDICO calls.

any extra as the timing equipment stops as soon as the subscriber puts the phone down.

Broadcasts
One important word of advice; try not to call a Coast Station on his primary working channel when a broadcast is near. Before calling, check in your almanac to see the time of the next broadcast from that station and if you are within, say, ten minutes, call on another channel. (Primary channels are the

first ones in the list in Appendix F). The reason for doing this is that if, for instance, a weather forecast is due on Channel 27 and a link call is in progress, the operator will have to break in as the forecast takes priority over commercial traffic. The operator will say:

THIS CHANNEL IS GOING TO BE TAKEN FOR A BROADCAST.
DO YOU WISH TO BE RECONNECTED AFTERWARDS?

If you have nearly finished there's no problem, but if you want to carry on, the operator will re-enter your boat's details into the computer and you will be reconnected after the broadcast. You will not be charged for the first three minutes of the reconnection. The big problem, of course, is that you will have had to sit through a broadcast which might be ten minutes long.

While we're on the subject of broadcasts, Coast Stations send weather forecasts, gale warnings and navigational warnings at the times shown in Appendix G. The operator will send the broadcast twice, once at conversation speed and once at dictation speed.

BT have a card which gives details of how to use Coast Stations and the services they offer, together with a map showing the position of all radio stations and their times of broadcast. A letter to your nearest station will produce one free of charge. As with the Coastguard, if you would like to see what happens when you make a link call, write to your nearest station and ask to have a look around. If you are a member of a yacht or boat club gather a group together. Station Managers will also be pleased to visit your club to answer any questions you might have on radio procedure.

Coast Stations cannot be used as a relay between two vessels out of line of sight range.

Calls from shore to ship

Calls can be made to yachts from the land by dialling 0800 378389. This puts you through to an operator at Portishead

Radio in Somerset who will take the details of your booking. Portishead is the central booking point for all R/T calls. If you do make calls to a boat, give the operator as much information as possible, including the correct spelling of the name (as mentioned earlier), the callsign of the vessel and roughly where it is. This will make it easier to call the boat through the correct station and will speed things up.

Once the details have been entered into the system the boat is immediately called on Channel 16. Further calls will be made after weather forecasts, navigation warnings and gale warnings. Coast Stations no longer broadcast separate traffic lists ie calls to boats. Shore to ship calls are billed to the telephone number of the person calling. If you hear your boat's name called by a Coast Station, reply direct on a working channel.

Automatic radio telephone

BT has introduced a new service called Autolink. It is an automatic system which means that you can dial a land number direct from your boat without having to go through the Coast Station operator. It uses the same channels as normal calls and requires an extra piece of equipment plugged into your VHF set. For it to work properly, the system needs to be set up correctly, a job that should be carried out by the company you buy the equipment from. This system also offers call scrambling for added security, and is charged by the minute instead of a three minute minimum. The Autolink equipment has to be registered with BT at which time you are issued with a PIN number. Up to 99 PIN numbers can be issued for each set and each number can have a choice of billing methods – UK telephone number, ships' Accounting Authority or BT Chargecard. There is no rental for the system, unlike cellular phones.

Autolink is only available in the from-ship direction.

If you do make use of this system you must take the same care as if you were making a conventional call, listen on the channel first.

More information on this service can be obtained from the address in Appendix H.

Marinas

Small craft registered in Britain have, in the past, been able to use a private channel, M (Channel 37) to communicate directly with marinas and yacht clubs. From 1 April 1989 changes were made to the use of this channel. The primary calling and working channel for marinas has been changed from 37 to 80, with 37 being relegated to use as an overload channel if 80 is busy or not yet available. However things are not quite that easy. Some marinas do not have Channel 80, which is Duplex, and still use 37 which is Simplex, so unless you know for certain which to use you'll have to find the right one by trial and error.

Channel M2 (161.425MHz) is for use as race control by yacht clubs, but again 37 can be used if M2 is busy or not available. These channels are unique to Britain and do not operate outside the UK nor can foreign vessels use them.

As these are private channels separate authority is needed to use them. Normally this is no problem and permission comes with your licence when the boat is first registered. If you find for some reason that you are not licensed to use this channel write to the Department of Trade and Industry. British marinas and yacht clubs are only licensed to operate on these channels, so all calls must be made on Channel M or 80 *not* 16.

As with most things, there are exceptions to the rule such as Brighton Marina, which must be called as Brighton Control on Channel 16 or Brighton Marina on Channel M.

The *Admiralty List of Radio Signals* (ALRS) Vol 6 will give you all the information you need including telephone numbers so that you have up to date information.

Port Radio Stations

Port Radio Stations are operated by harbour authorities. There is no compulsion to ask permission to enter or leave most ports. ALRS Vol 6 gives full details of the hours of watch, as few harbours maintain a 24 hour service. It also gives details of channels to use and the way to address your call. Normally it will be something like:

FALMOUTH HARBOUR RADIO
THIS IS YACHT NONSUCH
OVER

Some harbour authorities listen on Channel 16 and transfer to a working channel while others listen only on their working channels. The most common channels are 12 and 14 but check with ALRS Vol 6; it will save a lot of wasted breath.

You may use your radio for all services offered by BT Coast Stations while you are alongside in harbour provided you have permission from the local port authority but you are bound by local regulations regarding the use of radio near areas where hazardous cargo is worked. It is probably just as easy and cheap to go to a telephone box on the quay to make a call home.

You may also use your radio to receive messages from authorised broadcast stations intended for general reception, and to communicate with the port authorities. As with all calling, always listen for a minute or two before you call on a working channel in case there are shipping movements in progress. A common complaint from harbour masters is that people call without listening just at the moment when a ship is being berthed blotting out essential instructions to tugs.

Port information services

Vessel Traffic Services (VTS) are available on request from most port radio stations in major commercial harbours. Information broadcasts vary from local navigation warnings to tide heights. As frequencies vary it is best to look up the details in ALRS Vol 6. Southampton actually broadcasts this type of information for small craft on Channel 12 every even hour from 0600 to 2200 local time Friday to Sunday and Bank Holiday Mondays from Easter to 30 September.

Channels to avoid
Some of the channels which are listed as inter-ship should not be used as such under certain circumstances. In naval bases the Queen's Harbour Master is in charge and uses Channel 13, so in the Portsmouth, Weymouth, Plymouth and Rosyth areas do not use this channel. In the vicinity of major ports, Channel 9 is often used by pilot vessels and tugs, and in the Solent, Channel 10 is used for pollution control reporting.

River Thames
If you use the River Thames, information regarding the Thames Barrier is shown in ALRS Vol 6 and routine messages about the Barrier are broadcast by Gravesend Radio on Channel 12 every half hour, and by Woolwich Radio on Channel 14 every quarter past and quarter to the hour.

Information messages for the Thames in general are issued by the Thames Navigation Service and are broadcast by North Foreland, Hastings, Thames and Orfordness Radio on their working channels following an announcement on Channel 16.

Various other harbour authorities have their own rules and regulations and ALRS Vol 6 gives details of these along with frequencies.

Using VHF in harbour
One final point regarding ports and harbours. Many have high stone walls to which you moor and at low tide you may find yourself some way below the level of the quay. In such a position you may find it difficult to communicate with anyone outside your immediate vicinity by radio, as VHF waves do not travel through solid objects such as walls. There is little you can do about this apart from moving outside the harbour.

Ship to ship calls

One of the nice things about having a radio on a boat is that you can contact other boats around you. It is not practical, however, to hail every passing yacht for a chat. Hopefully you will rarely hear such calls as:

AHOY THERE. WHITE YACHT WITH BLUE SAIL APPROACHING ME
HOW DO YOU READ?
OVER

BLACK HULLED CARGO SHIP TWO MILES ON MY PORT BOW
THIS IS MV NONSUCH

These sorts of calls are not only meaningless, they also contravene the regulation which states that you must use both vessels' names when making a call. Moreover, when making this type of blind call you don't even know if the boat you are calling has a radio switched on, so keep ship to ship calls to boats you know are listening.

If you want to call another vessel the normal procedure is to call on Channel 16 and transfer to an intership working channel designated by the vessel being called. Make the call brief:

YACHT NONSUCH NONSUCH NONSUCH
THIS IS YACHT RAINBOW RAINBOW
OVER

Of course, if you change to a channel and find someone already talking there you must go back to Channel 16 and talk to the other party who will choose another channel to transfer to. It is permissible to call direct on intership channels, but you will obviously have to prearrange this.

Once you have moved to the working channel keep your conversation as brief as possible; the idea of these channels is to pass information rather than to have a cosy chat.

Radio lighthouses

There are only two of these stations still working, one at Anvil Point near Swanage, the other at Scratchell Bay on the Isle of Wight near the Needles. They transmit a rotating directional signal on Channel 88 consisting of a tone which is broken down into a series of beats, each beat corresponding to a radial at intervals of 2. You count the number of beats and read off the bearing of the lighthouse from seaward from a conversion chart. The volume of the tone decreases as the null radial is approached and increases again following the null. Anvil Point's sector is 247°-007° and Scratchell Bay 337°-097°. Full details of these stations are given in ALRS Vol 2 and yachtsman's almanacs.

Each station has a two letter callsign and the whole transmission cycle takes one minute with a one minute break (during which the other transmits) before it starts again.

The cycle is broken down into:

0.1 secs silence
3.2 secs identification
0.3 secs digital data
0.1 secs silence
32.0 secs beats
1.0 secs silence
0.1 secs digital data
14.1 secs silence

The only part of this that you are really interested in is the beats; the digital data is of no importance to the yachtsman.

Beats 10,20,30,40,50,60 are emphasised by a change in the tone. Table 2 gives an example of a conversion table.

If, for example, you had counted 52 beats from the station, you would look up the conversion table in your almanac and see that the bearing of the lighthouse from seaward was 337.

The use of VHF for these beacons is only temporary, and eventually it is planned to use special frequencies outside the VHF RT band which will not be received by normal radio telephone equipment.

TABLE 2

Typical table for obtaining bearings from a Radio Lighthouse
Bearing of lighthouse from seaward in degrees

Count of Beats	0	1	2	3	4	5	6	7	8	9
0								247	249	251
10	253	255	257	259	261	263	265	267	269	271
20	273	275	277	279	281	283	285	287	289	291
30	293	295	297	299	301	303	305	307	309	311
40	313	315	317	319	321	323	325	327	329	331
50	333	335	337	339	341	343	345	347	349	351
60	353	355	357	359	001	003	005	007		
70										

Publications

We have talked quite a bit about the *Admiralty List of Radio Signals*, but what exactly is it? It is a series of paperback books published by the Hydrographer of the Navy which you can buy from any agent who sells Admiralty charts. These give details of every radio station in the world that deals with ships. There are six volumes in the series, some of which have two parts. You are not likely to need them all; *Volume One part one*, which gives details of Coast Stations in Britain and Europe, *Volume Three* detailing weather forecasts, and *Volume Six part one* which covers VHF stations such as marinas and ports are probably the most useful. The main problem is that they are not cheap and they are updated each week by the Hydrographer, a task which, apart from being prohibitively expensive, is not really practical for the average yachtsman. Despite the drawbacks they are a most useful source of information.

Almanacs

The various yachtsman's almanacs give most of the details that you will need about the various types of stations you'll be using, but the general information contained in the ALRS will be missing and the almanacs are not updated until the following year.

Meteorological Office

The Met Office issues a useful booklet called *Weather Services for Shipping*, outlining their services and containing two rub clean plastic cards on which you can take down details of forecasts and gale warnings. Sea areas and reporting stations are printed on them, with columns for wind, sea state and visibility. It saves trying to find a piece of paper and something to write with when taking down the forecast, and then trying to decipher your handwriting afterwards. You can obtain a copy of this useful booklet from the Met Office at the address in Appendix H.

Distress, urgency, medico and safety

The most important use of radio at sea is for safety. There are three areas that concern us, Distress, Urgency and Safety. We will deal with each in turn.

Distress

For our purposes the only distress channel that we need worry about is Channel 16. This is monitored by the Coastguard 24 hours a day for distress calls. British Telecom Coast Radio Stations have no obligation to listen on this channel.

Hopefully, you will never be in distress yourself, but what if you do find yourself in trouble or what if you hear someone else with a problem? It may seem obvious but it is worth repeating that a distress call must not be made unless the crew or the craft itself is in distress. At the beginning of each sailing season Channel 16 has a spate of MAYDAY calls. Each time the Coastguard hears the word MAYDAY they must act as if it were a genuine distress. At the time they do not know whether it is a hoax or not, and a great deal of time, effort and money can be wasted in dealing with this sort of call. Having said that, every vessel at sea is under a legal obligation to answer a distress call. The rules state that only the master of the ship, in our case the skipper, shall order the sending of a distress call and he must be satisfied that:

The craft or a member of the crew is threatened by grave and imminent danger and requires immediate assistance

Once any danger is over the skipper must send a message revoking the distress working (see later).

So, what do we do if we are in distress ourselves? It is easy to say, 'Don't panic' but a clear head obviously helps. First of all, do we really need to send a distress message? How do you know if you're in distress or just in a spot of bother? It's not always easy for someone with a problem in the middle of the briny to think this through.

Are you really in distress?

To give you some idea, picture this if you will. You are on a motor cruiser ten miles offshore on a sunny summer's day. There is little wind and nothing around you. Your engine stops and you cannot get it going. Are you in distress?

To you, at the time, it may well seem so. There you are, ten miles offshore with no apparent means of getting to port. However, if we take the criteria set out earlier we will find that neither the vessel nor any of its crew is in imminent danger; it is not going to sink or strike rocks. In this situation you do require assistance but not necessarily immediately. In this situation you would make a PAN broadcast on Channel 16 and tell the Coastguard of your problem.

If we take the same set of circumstances but substitute an onshore Force eight gale which would soon have you on the rocks, your craft is most definitely in grave and imminent danger. You now have a distress on your hands. What do you do?

Distress call and message

Check your set is switched on and is on high power. Check that you are tuned to Channel 16. Press the PTT switch and, talking slowly and distinctly, make the distress call which consists of:

- MAYDAY three times.
- Vessel's name or call sign three times.

If you are a small craft it helps the Coastguard if you prefix the name with 'Yacht' or 'motor cruiser'—this identifies the type of vessel involved from the outset. Once the initial call has been made you must then impart the essential information in a specific order:

- MAYDAY once and the vessel's name or call sign once.
- Give the vessel's position as accurately as possible in latitude and longitude or as a true bearing and distance *from* a recognisable geographical point.
- Give the nature of distress and help needed.
- Give the total number of persons on board.
- Any other essential information.
- Ask for reply by saying OVER

An example of the call and message is as follows:

Call:
MAYDAY MAYDAY MAYDAY
THIS IS
YACHT NONSUCH YACHT NONSUCH YACHT NONSUCH

Message:
MAYDAY YACHT NONSUCH
POSITION THREE MILES WEST OF LONGSHIPS LIGHTHOUSE
STRUCK ROCK. TAKING IN WATER
REQUIRE IMMEDIATE ASSISTANCE
FOUR PEOPLE ON BOARD
OVER

Position When giving a true bearing, make sure it is from a *known* geographical point. If you use a local name the Coastguard may not know exactly where you are.

Nature of distress Say whether you are sinking, being swept on to rocks or are on fire etc.

Assistance required Give the right emphasis - if you are actually sinking or there is a serious fire you will want IMMEDIATE ASSISTANCE.

Number of people on board Make sure you count yourself.

Any other information Example: I WILL FIRE A RED FLARE/I WILL ACTIVATE MY EPIRB.

Give only essential information in your initial call and message then release the PTT switch and listen for a reply. Once you have sent the message you should expect an immediate response. If you don't get one check that your set is working and try again. If there is still no reply, try another channel such as 6 or 8.

Once you have received a reply from the Coastguard he will ask for any further information he requires and will rebroadcast your message word for word using MAYDAY RELAY so that other vessels in the area know of your plight, and decide on the type of assistance you need. Note down everything he tells you and do as you are told. He may rebroadcast your details like this:

MAYDAY RELAY MAYDAY RELAY MAYDAY RELAY
THIS IS FALMOUTH COASTGUARD FALMOUTH COASTGUARD
FALMOUTH COASTGUARD
FOLLOWING RECEIVED FROM YACHT NONSUCH
AT ONE THREE ZERO ZERO
BEGINS MAYDAY MAYDAY MAYDAY ... (They will follow this with the message word for word that you sent.)
THIS IS FALMOUTH COASTGUARD
OUT

The Coastguard has an adhesive notice which gives MAYDAY call information which you can stick on the bulkhead next to the radio.

Operations Room at Falmouth Coastguard showing (right) the VHF direction finding equipment. The operator is entering information in a computerised logging and data retrieval system which is used extensively during casualty working.

Cancelling a MAYDAY or reducing a MAYDAY to a PAN.

If your circumstances change, perhaps the wind changes direction and you are no longer being blown on to rocks or you get your engine going and can make your own way to port, you must advise the Coastguard that you are no longer in danger. If you feel that everything is under control and there is no need for the lifeboat or helicopter to continue to you, you can tell the Coastguard to cancel the MAYDAY. If you are not confident that your engine will get you to port or if you think the weather may change again, you can ask them to downgrade the MAYDAY to a PAN. Either way, the method of calling is the same:

> MAYDAY FALMOUTH COASTGUARD
> THIS IS YACHT NONSUCH
> I'VE GOT MY ENGINE GOING NOW AND I THINK I CAN
> MAKE IT TO PENZANCE. I AM IN NO FURTHER DANGER
> PLEASE CANCEL MAYDAY
> OVER

or:

> MAYDAY FALMOUTH COASTGUARD
> THIS IS YACHT NONSUCH
> I'VE GOT MY ENGINE GOING NOW BUT I'M NOT CONFIDENT THAT
> IT WILL KEEP GOING
> I'M IN NO IMMEDIATE DANGER
> PLEASE REDUCE MAYDAY TO PAN
> OVER

Even if you decide to cancel the MAYDAY it is almost certain that the Coastguard will ask you to call him every so often so that he can monitor your progress.

Acknowledging a distress message
What happens if you hear someone else broadcast a distress message? It will most probably be heard and acknowledged by a Coastguard station who will take all necessary action. In this case you should make a note of the message and check to see if you are anywhere near the position of the casualty and therefore able to help. If you are only a few miles away you should call the Coastguard, give them your position and ask if they require you to proceed. (The rest will follow automatically.)

> MAYDAY FALMOUTH COASTGUARD
> THIS IS YACHT SKYLARK
> MY POSITION IS THREE MILES WEST OF BLACK HEAD
> DO YOU WISH ME TO PROCEED
> OVER

> MAYDAY YACHT SKYLARK
> THIS IS FALMOUTH COASTGUARD
> WOULD YOU START PROCEEDING TO THE CASUALTY AND
> GIVE ME AN ETA PLEASE
> OVER

MAYDAY FALMOUTH COASTGUARD
THIS IS YACHT SKYLARK
ROGER. AM PROCEEDING. WILL REVERT WITH MY ETA
OVER

This exchange would continue until the Coastguard has all the information he needs. Then he would make another broadcast giving all the original information regarding the name and position of the casualty but adding:

YACHT SKYLARK PROCEEDING. ETA ONE THREE TWO ZERO.
PENLEE LIFEBOAT LAUNCHED.
ETA ONE THREE TWO FIVE

If you can establish communication with the stricken vessel, so much the better.

MAYDAY YACHT NONSUCH NONSUCH NONSUCH
THIS IS YACHT SKYLARK SKYLARK SKYLARK
MY POSITION TWO MILES SOUTH OF TATER DU
WILL REACH YOU AT APPROXIMATELY ONE THREE TWO ZERO
OVER

Nonsuch should reply something this:

MAYDAY YACHT SKYLARK
THIS IS NONSUCH
UNDERSTOOD
STANDING BY THIS CHANNEL

If you have difficulty finding him, you can always call again using the same format as above to ask him to fire a flare or to see if he can see you.

What if a craft calls for help and you seem to be the only one to have heard him? This is very unlikely but does happen occasionally, and obviously puts you on the spot. Whenever you hear the word MAYDAY spoken, write down everything that is said. In this situation it is particularly important. Once the distress message has been completed wait a few moments to see if anyone does answer. If there is no reply and you know that it is a small craft to which you could render assistance, you should acknowledge the message in the following way:

MAYDAY
YACHT NONSUCH NONSUCH NONSUCH
THIS IS YACHT SKYLARK SKYLARK SKYLARK
RECEIVED MAYDAY

Immediately you have acknowledged the call you must rebroadcast it using MAYDAY RELAY:

MAYDAY RELAY MAYDAY RELAY MAYDAY RELAY
THIS IS YACHT SKYLARK SKYLARK SKYLARK
FOLLOWING RECEIVED FROM YACHT NONSUCH
AT ONE THREE ZERO ZERO
BEGINS MAYDAY MAYDAY MAYDAY (Follow this with the message
word for word that the striken yacht has already broadcast)
MESSAGE ENDS
OVER

If you are in a position to assist you must then transmit a follow-up message to the casualty giving your position and the approximate time you will reach him:

MAYDAY NONSUCH NONSUCH NONSUCH
THIS IS SKYLARK SKYLARK SKYLARK
MY POSITION TWO MILES SOUTH OF TATER DU
WILL REACH YOU AT APPROXIMATELY ONE THREE TWO ZERO
OVER

If the casualty is able he should acknowledge your message.

The question of how much you can assist a casualty does not have an easy answer. If you know that it is a small craft or one with only a few people on board there is no real problem, but what if it is larger? A small yacht or motor cruiser is not likely to be of much use although, of course, any assistance is better than none. In these circumstances by the time a decision has to be made about proceeding, the Coastguard should have become involved and will make the decision for you.

If no-one replies to a distress call you must make all effort to contact the Coastguard or a Coast Station. This could be by calling them yourself or calling a commercial ship, if you can see one near you with more powerful equipment who would relay the message.

The word 'proceeding' can have more than one interpretation. A German cargo ship on hearing a MAYDAY RELAY broadcast by a Coast Station immediately acknowledged it just as the book says. The operator at the Coast Station was pretty certain that the ship was nowhere near the casualty but went through the procedures. 'Are you proceeding?' he asked the ship. 'Yes,' was the reply. 'Where to?' 'To Hamburg.'

Distress calls from other than the casualty

Are there any occasions when someone other than the casualty can make a distress call? The simple answer is, Yes.

There is, of course, the situation above where no one has acknowledged the call, but there are two others:

- If the casualty cannot broadcast itself.
- If further help is necessary.

In both cases the call MAYDAY RELAY must be used.

Control of distress

The question of who is in control of matters during a distress situation is important. In theory it is the vessel in distress, but in practice he has enough to do without worrying about co-ordinating things, so it is normally the Coastguard who takes control because he has everything he needs to render assistance at his fingertips.

Silence during distress

During a distress situation radio silence is imposed, and anyone hearing SEELONCE MAYDAY should immediately stop transmitting. If a station near to the distress feels that it is essential to impose radio silence it should use SEELONCE DISTRESS although this should only be used in exceptional cases. You may hear:

MAYDAY
SEELONCE DISTRESS SEELONCE DISTRESS SEELONCE DISTRESS
THIS IS YACHT SKYLARK SKYLARK
OUT

Completion of distress

When the station controlling the distress feels that the situation is under control and complete radio silence is no longer required he can allow restricted use of Channel 16 by using

PRUDONCE:

MAYDAY
ALL STATIONS ALL STATIONS ALL STATIONS
THIS IS FALMOUTH COASTGUARD
TIME ONE THREE FOUR FIVE
YACHT NONSUCH
PRUDONCE
OUT

PRUDONCE means that restricted working may be carried out and that a full MAYDAY could be re-imposed at any time. Keep calls on Channel 16 to a minimum and preferably only to those affecting Distress, Urgency and Safety. As always, listen carefully before you transmit to make sure no distress working is in progress.

When distress working has been completed the controlling station will announce this using the words SEELONCE FINEE:

MAYDAY
ALL STATIONS ALL STATIONS ALL STATIONS
THIS IS FALMOUTH COASTGUARD
TIME ONE FOUR ZERO ZERO
YACHT NONSUCH
SEELONCE FINEE

Procedure guide

There might be a time when you get into distress when the only person on board who knows how to use the radio is unable to do so. What do you do then?

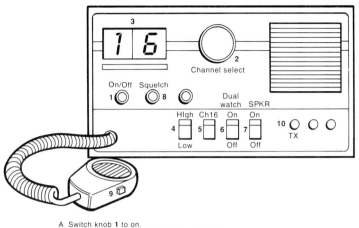

A Switch knob **1** to on.
B Turn knob **2** until 16 appears in window **3**.
C Put switch **4** to high.
D Put switch **5** to Ch 16.
E Put switch **6** to Off.
F Put switch **7** to On.
G Turn knob **8** until noise in speaker just disappears.
H Pick up microphone, press knob **9** on side and see if light **10** is lit. This indicates that you are transmitting.
I Hold microphone about 6 inches from your mouth and speak slowly and steadily.
J Make your distress call and message, referring to the example on the card.

Fig 10 How to send a distress message

On merchant ships the emergency radio transmitter has a procedure guide attached to it showing the front of the equipment with all the knobs and switches labelled, and a step by step guide on how to use the set. Of course this type of radio is more complicated than a VHF, but it might be a good idea to prepare a similar card for your set. An example is given in Figure 10. You could put another card next to it giving an example of how to make a distress call and message.

Emergency position indicating beacons (EPIRB)

An EPIRB is basically a homing beacon which can be set off by a mariner in distress. There are three types which operate on one of these frequencies: 121.5MHz which can be received by civil aircraft and satellites, 243MHz which can be picked up only by military aircraft, and 406MHz which can be picked up only by satellites.

The 406MHz type is the newest and most preferred type as the satellite can not only pick up the signals and redirect them to a Coastguard station such as Falmouth but can give a position and even the name of the vessel and nature of the emergency. Once the Coastguard station receives a report of an EPIRB going off a MAYDAY broadcast is initiated. The content of the broadcast varies but normally asks vessels in the area to check their EPIRBs to make sure they are not transmitting accidentally, and requesting ships to keep a sharp lookout for any sign of a vessel in distress. Aircraft such as the RAF Nimrod can then pin-point the vessel with its direction-finding eqiupment.

EPIRBs require a licence and details can be obtained from the Department of Trade and Industry at the address in Appendix H. If you do buy one, store it carefully so that it will not be set off accidentally and if it is deliberately activated do not switch it off until the emergency is over.

It is important to realise that EPIRBs are not a substitute for a conventional VHF set and they must only be used for distress purposes. A ship in the English Channel picked up a broadcast from a Coast Station about an EPIRB and reported that he could hear it very well. The captain started to search for the elusive beacon convinced that the vessel in distress was nearby. It was some time later that he found that it was his own that had somehow fallen over the side, had been activated and was being towed along by the ship. There were red faces all round!

Urgency

If there is no immediate danger to your craft and assistance is not required immediately the Urgency signal should be used. This consists of the spoken word PAN and is transmitted on

Channel 16. This indicates that you have a very urgent message to transmit regarding the safety of your craft and it has priority over all traffic except distress.

The following example shows that although you are in trouble there is no immediate danger to your craft.

PAN PAN PAN PAN PAN PAN
ALL STATIONS ALL STATIONS ALL STATIONS
THIS IS MOTOR CRUISER NONSUCH NONSUCH NONSUCH
ONE EIGHT ZERO FROM LONGSHIPS LIGHT, THREE MILES
COMPLETE ENGINE FAILURE. DRIFTING SOUTH AT THREE KNOTS
REQUIRE TOW URGENTLY
OVER

As in the case of distress, the Coastguard should answer you and make arrangements for assistance.

If you see a vessel nearby who would be able to assist, you can address your call to him rather than all ships.

Medico

There are two distinct areas where medicos are concerned and it depends on which category you fall into (if you pardon the pun) as to whom you contact. If you need assistance, the Coastguard will help, while if you want advice, BT Coast Stations are the ones to contact. There is often confusion as to exactly which is which.

Medical assistance
If you have someone on board who is obviously injured with, say, a broken arm or leg, then it is fairly obvious that the casualty should be transferred to shore as quickly as possible. In this case you should call the Coastguard on Channel 16 using the PAN MEDICO signal.

PAN PAN MEDICO PAN PAN MEDICO PAN PAN MEDICO
FALMOUTH COASTGUARD FALMOUTH COASTGUARD FALMOUTH
COASTGUARD
THIS IS YACHT NONSUCH NONSUCH NONSUCH
I REQUIRE MEDICAL ASSISTANCE
OVER

The Coastguard will ask you for information on the problem and arrange help. You will almost certainly have to talk to a doctor first as he is the only person who can authorise evacuation. The Coastguard cannot make this decision without his say-so and the next section shows you how to make a call to a doctor.

Medical advice
If you have someone on board with stomach pains or who has been hit by the boom and has a headache, the first thing you will need is advice, and will need to make a link call to a doctor through a Coast Station.

The quickest way to do this is to call the Coastguard on Channel 16 using the PAN MEDICO signal as before but, instead of saying you require assistance, you say you need medical advice. The Coastguard will ask you for your position, will contact Lands End Radio or Stonehaven Radio who co-ordinate PAN MEDICOS, and come back with a clear working channel at your nearest Coast Station. By the time you have changed channels, an operator will have your details and will be waiting for you. Don't start giving details to the operator; he will connect you to a doctor. These calls are free.

Hold on a minute! I hear you say. Earlier you told us to call a Coast Station direct on a working channel. Now you're telling us to call the Coastguard for medical advice on Channel 16. Why can't I call the Coast Station direct? The simple answer is that if you call a Coast Station direct you will go into the general mêlée of things and could wait a few minutes before anyone answers you, and the operator will not know that you have a PAN MEDICO until you tell him. You could try calling the nearest Coast Station on Channel 16 but there is the possibility that the station may not be staffed and your call will go unheard.

Obviously you want as little delay as possible. Calling the Coastguard may seem a long winded way of going about things but it really is the quickest.

Giving details
Doctors who deal with PAN MEDICOS say that one of the major problems they face is lack of information about the patient. Saying, 'I've got someone with stomach ache, what should I do?' is no use. It is very difficult to make a diagnosis when you can't see the patient. Try to get information covering the following:

- Description of patient (male/female, age)
- Where the symptoms are (chest/back/leg)
- Any general symptoms (sharp pain/dull ache)
- Any particular symptoms (pain increased on breathing/swallowing is painful)
- Previous health (Do they suffer from anything that might be causing the symptoms? Are they taking medication for anything?)

Write down as much as you can; it will help the doctor make a faster diagnosis and he will not have to ask you so many questions. Make sure you know what sort of medication you have on board; the doctor may well ask you.

Here is an example of a PAN MEDICO call:

'I have a patient, male, aged 31 years. He has been ill for three hours and is in severe pain in area of left kidney. Pain is increased by hand pressure. He is sweating, has had no previous illness and is not taking medication.'

Some idea of his temperature and pulse would help if you are able to take either. The Coast Station Radio Officer will be monitoring the call and, from experience, will have a good idea whether the patient will need evacuation. The Coast Station will keep the Coastguard advised of the situation but as we have said, the final decision on whether to take a patient off lies with the doctor. If this is the case, the Coastguard will be advised and will arrange everything. Once you have finished the call, go back to Channel 16 and call the Coastguard. He will move you to a working channel and tell you when the lifeboat or helicopter will arrive. It may be that you are close enough to a port to divert and land the patient to an ambulance.

Don't ask the Coastguard for medical advice because they have no means of connecting you to the telephone system. I would not use a cellular telephone either as the coast is not fully covered by cellular radio and if you did get through you would be charged for the call. You would also need to know the telephone number of a doctor and, should he decide that the patient required evacuation, he would have to advise the Coastguard and you would have no means of talking to the helicopter or lifeboat.

Things are often not always as bad as they seem however. Take the fellow who suddenly started having pains in the chest and a tingling up one arm into the face. He ended up in the casualty unit of a hospital in double quick time. A heart attack? Well, not exactly. He had bought a new expanding strap for his watch which was too tight. It cut off the blood supply to his wrist causing the tingling. He had also eaten two jam doughnuts one after the other with his morning coffee which gave him chronic indigestion.

Safety

The SAFETY signal consists of the spoken word SAY-CUREETAY (SECURITE) and is used to prefix a message containing navigational or meteorological information.

The initial call is sent on Channel 16 but the message itself must be sent on a working channel. Normally you will hear Coast Stations using this signal to prefix their navigational or gale warnings, but small craft owners can use it if, for instance, they are sailing in a narrow channel and come across a navigational hazard such as a floating container or log which they consider to be a danger to other vessels. It might take this form:

SAYCUREETAY SAYCUREETAY SAYCUREETAY
ALL STATIONS ALL STATIONS ALL STATIONS
THIS IS LANDS END RADIO LANDS END RADIO LANDS END RADIO
FOR NAVIGATIONAL WARNINGS LISTEN CHANNEL TWO SEVEN

(on Channel 27)

SAYCUREETAY SAYCUREETAY SAYCUREETAY
ALL STATIONS ALL STATIONS ALL STATIONS THIS IS
LANDS END RADIO LANDS END RADIO LANDS END RADIO
NAVIGATIONAL WARNING WHISKEY ZULU THREE SIX FOUR
LONGSHIPS LIGHTHOUSE. FOG SIGNAL INOPERATIVE

As with the Urgency signal, the Safety signal is normally directed to all stations but can be used to one particular station if necessary.

To end this chapter here's a true story for you to ponder. It's a bright sunny morning. A charter fishing boat is alongside a quay, its party of eager fishermen embarking. However, no sooner has the boat left the quay than one of the party feels seasick, and by the time they reach the harbour entrance, some hundred yards away, he is feeling very sorry for himself. If you were skipper of this boat what would you do at this point? Turn around and put him ashore?

In this case the skipper carried on and as the day progressed the man's condition became worse until eventually after six hours it was so bad that he was almost unconscious and those on board began to worry. The skipper now asked for assistance, a helicopter was scrambled and the casualty taken to hospital where he made a full recovery. The question later asked was why the man had been allowed to lie around, obviously in distress, for so long before assistance was called. As it happened everything turned out well, but another hour might have resulted in a different outcome.

Remember, in a distress *you can never do too much.*

Misuse of VHF radio

If you listen to a marine VHF for any length of time you'll hear all sorts of banter, some good, some very bad and some illegal. Even professionals have been heard to make the odd faux pas. Hopefully once you have your licence to operate you will want to be as professional as possible when using your equipment and this chapter outlines some of the things that you should be doing and those that you most definitely should not.

Channel 16

Probably the main area of misuse concerns unnecessary interference on Channel 16 which, of course, is for distress and calling purposes only. Use of this channel should be restricted to establishing contact with another vessel or shore station. Once this has been done, both parties must transfer to a working channel as quickly as possible.

Early in the year, when boats start coming out of mothballs and the excitement of the coming sailing season starts to permeate through the boating fraternity, the 'silly season' starts.

It begins with a few noises on Channel 16, builds up to giggles and someone doing an impersonation of Frank Sinatra, climaxing with someone calling MAYDAY. On the whole, few of these transmissions are malicious but all require looking into.

Let's take an example. It's just before six o'clock in the evening and two fishing boats report to the Coastguard that they have heard the word MAYDAY spoken once on Channel 16. The Coastguard initiates a PAN broadcast asking other vessels to report if they have heard this signal. Around seven o'clock, the Coastguards are told by another Coastguard station that they had heard a MAYDAY call with laughter and children's voices in the background. Having heard nothing else the PAN is cancelled at seven-thirty pm.

The majority of such calls are from children who have been left alone on the boat while mum and dad go ashore or on to someone else's boat. A VHF set is the easiest thing in the world to operate but you must be responsible and not leave children alone, especially with the set switched on. If we take the situation above we can see that not only did the call waste an hour and a half of Coastguard time but various regulations had been broken which, had the culprits been found, could have led to prosecution, a fine and loss of licence.

We must assume that Dad, who we'll say has the licence to operate, was not on board so the transmissions were not authorised by the person in charge of the equipment and the set was operated by unauthorised persons, namely the children. By messing around, transmissions were made without identifying the vessel and a false MAYDAY was sent. So you can see that from just one incident at least four breaches of regulations were made.

Overcalling

If the station you want to communicate with does not answer, do not call over and over. There must be a reason why he doesn't answer; he may not have his radio on, you might be out of range or he might be doing something else. Wait *at least three minutes* before trying again and before you do, check that the set is switched on, the gain is up, the squelch correctly set and you are on the right channel.

It is not only bad operating practice; it is illegal, and if a Coastguard or Coast Station hears you they may well file an infringement report with the Department of Trade Inspectors.

The only time you can break the three minute rule is if you are in distress. Allied to this, if you hear another boat or shore station calling and you're not sure they were calling you, wait a few minutes. If they really were trying to contact you they will call again. There is no need to reply, 'Was anyone calling me?'

Making contact

Have you ever been to a party where 'know-it-all' Bloggs just can't be left out of any conversation even if it means butting in? It happens in radio as well. There are those people who cannot resist trying to break in on intership calls and either keep pressing their PTT switch, trying to attract attention, or go the whole hog and start calling one of the boats when a conversation is going on. If you hear someone you know on the air, wait until the conversation has finished or there is a break before calling.

'Calling Uncle Joe. This is Bert here' is not allowed, even if your Uncle Joe is on the boat you are calling. You must always use the boat's name or callsign when calling another station. Remember, it is an offence to make calls without identifying yourself. It is also illegal to use christian names or other unauthorised identification in lieu of the vessel's name or callsign. Skippers of fishing boats can often be heard, 'Silver Fish Silver Fish Aquarius Aquarius. Are you about Jim?' While he has used both vessel's names it is not really the proper way to call another boat.

Language

Bad language is not normally a problem with small boat owners, but of course it is forbidden to swear on the air. Trawler skippers again seem to be the exception to the rule and some very salty language can be heard when they are about. Be warned!

Closing down your station

You must not switch your radio off if you are involved in Distress, Safety or Urgency working before finishing all communications relating to that working. Neither must you close down if you are in the middle of exchanging traffic with a Coast Station or other vessels which have indicated that they want to contact you.

Broadcasting

Broadcasting means to transmit without expecting a reply. 'All Ships' messages are an exception to this and the rule really applies to those people who, for reasons best known to themselves, feel that they should broadcast music on Channel 16.

You must not broadcast messages which are intended for people ashore except through a Coast Station.

Secrecy

You must not divulge any information that you might come across while listening to link calls or from reading telegrams and it is forbidden to receive traffic which is not destined for your station. If you come upon this sort of information by accident you must not divulge even its existence.

Avoiding interference

One of the main faults with the new (and not so new) users of VHF is that they often open their mouths without engaging their brains. Do not switch on your set and immediately start calling. There might be other people using the frequency; there might be distress working going on which you will interrupt. *Always listen on Channel 16 for three or four minutes* before you start your business.

Channels

Always use the correct channel for the type of call you are making. Make your initial call to the Coastguard on Channel 16, and call a Coast Station for a link call direct on a working channel.

Repetition

'Nonsuch this is Jasmine. I have a message for you. Repeat I have a message for you.' This is a hang up from those old black and white films where everything was said twice for effect. Modern equipment is better designed than the old valve sets, which were often quite noisy. If your contact does not understand something he will soon tell you.

Over and out

What precisely does 'Over and Out' mean? It's something else that comes from the film world. It certainly does not mean that you are ending the conversation. If you look at it logically 'Over' is inviting the other party to say something while 'Out' means the end of the conversation. You can't do both.

Coast Stations

Do not ask someone ashore to make link calls for you, using them as a relay, or ask the Coastguard for a link call. Only BT Coast Stations are allowed to connect link calls; they are the only stations with equipment capable of connecting you to the telephone network.

When you are working a Coast Station, call on one channel and once you hear the pips stay on that channel. Some people have the annoying habit of getting the pips on one channel, waiting a few seconds and then calling again on another channel on the off chance that they will be answered more quickly there. The system does not work like that. Calls are answered in time order. Jumping around from channel to channel is a certain way of raising the blood pressure of even the mildest mannered Radio Officer. The same thing goes at the end of a call. Stay on the channel until the operator gives you the duration. If you go to another channel it will almost certainly be another operator that answers and he will not have the details of the call. As mentioned earlier, he may even be at another station. Another thing that is likely to drive an operator wild is someone asking for a repeat of the weather forecast or gale warning five minutes after it has been broadcast. If you want a forecast, check to see what time a Coast Station or Coastguard is going to send it and make sure you are listening at that time.

When you have finished making a call, always check to make sure that you have not left your transmitter on. This quite often happens and all that can be heard on Channel 16 are the sounds of people moving around, the clinking of glasses or the engine chugging away in the background. A few years ago, the cricket commentators on Radio 3 had to ask ships in the English Channel to check that they had not left their VHF sets on as all anyone in that area could hear on Channel 16 was the Test match commentary.

Everything described in this chapter has happened at one time or another. A little common sense, some thought and confidence will make you feel and sound professional.

Department of Trade Radio Interference Officers

These gentlemen are a somewhat mysterious breed. They are the same people who operate television detector vans and who check on illegal radio stations. They have the authority to carry out spot checks on radio stations of boats and can ask to see the licence for the equipment and your authority to operate. They can check your equipment and, if necessary, remove channels that you should not have. Even lifeboats and harbour masters have fallen foul of these gentlemen from time to time.

If your documents or equipment do not meet all regulations, they have the power to bring a prosecution against you. Be warned; they do occasionally have a blitz in harbours and marinas.

Alternatives: Citizens Band Radio and mobile telephones

Ok, so we've gone through the pros and cons of VHF radio on small boats, but are there any other methods of ship to shore communication which could be used, perhaps more easily and with less red tape? The simple answer is, Yes. I would qualify that with the fact that they do have limitations for the boat owner. Two means of ship to shore contact spring to mind. CB radio and cellular telephones. Neither is a substitute for VHF and neither should be relied on for distress purposes.

Citizens Band Radio

Once CB was legalised there was a rush to buy sets and all sorts of clubs were started. This initial enthusiasm died down and now just the hard core clubs remain. What exactly is CB? Well it's the use of radio in the 27MHz high frequency band and the 934MHz UHF band using frequency modulation, the same as VHF.

The 27 MHz frequencies are the most popular, mainly because of the lower cost of equipment. The band is divided into forty channels with a legal maximum transmitting power of 4 watts. Some people add power amplifiers or burners which increase the output power of the transmitter but this is illegal. You can use up to three sets with one licence which is obtainable at any Post Office. There is no exam to pass. The range of these sets will be slightly longer than VHF due to the lower frequencies being used and the quality of signal is just as good. Only speech may be transmitted. Before the 27 MHz FM service was legalised there were many 27 MHz AM sets being used. Some of these are still available but it is illegal to use them, and any set you buy should have CB 27/81 or 934/81 stamped on it.

What about its use in a marine environment? Equipment specifically designed or modified for use on boats is limited. Most are designed to act as base stations in a house or for fitting in cars, and many could be installed on a boat using standard car fittings. The problem is that a marine atmosphere is naturally damp and salty, and such conditions will play havoc with electronic equipment. I would not recommend buying such equipment for a boat unless you could take it out at the end of each trip. There are marinised sets available which are said to be waterproof, meaning that the circuit boards are lacquered and the outer casing is sealed. If you are thinking about CB this is the type to go for.

The equipment itself is mostly the same size as a VHF set. They have integral speakers, a hand held microphone with PTT switch and most of the knobs a VHF set has. One additional feature is a signal strength meter. This shows roughly how much power is being radiated when you transmit and the input level of the signal when you are receiving.

The same care and attention must be given to installing these sets as with VHF. The correct aerial must be used and it must be tuned to the transmitter. This is where the signal strength meter comes in. Whoever installs the set must tune the transmitter for maximum deflection on the meter. At this point you have most power going out. As with VHF there are various types of aerial available but again buy the best you can afford and make sure it is correctly fitted. Your normal 12V supply should be satisfactory to power the set. And as with VHF, when it comes to quality you get what you pay for.

As was said earlier, CB is not a substitute for VHF. It is a low cost way of communicating and it has its uses, but neither the Coastguard or British Telecom Coast Stations monitor CB frequencies. There is a monitoring system on Channel 9 but there is no guarantee that anyone is listening, nor is there any guarantee that if someone hears a MAYDAY call they will know what to do, although CB has played a part in marine rescues. Assuming you are heard, and the authorities advised, you will not be able to talk with any of the rescue services as neither RNLI lifeboats nor Search and Rescue helicopters are fitted with CB.

Apart from Channel 9, Channel 14 is the general calling channel. As with VHF you transfer to another, free, channel to conduct your conversation. Channel 19 is the one most often used by long distance lorry drivers.

CB is essentially a speech only system; it is illegal to advertise, transmit abusive language, transmit music or solicit goods or services. As a backup to VHF and if all you want to do is have a chat with friends, CB can play a useful part in keeping the VHF intership channels clear of idle chit-chat.

Cellular telephones

The other, perhaps more sophisticated, but definitely more expensive way of communicating is by using cellular telephones, the most common examples of which are car phones. There are three types available.

1 Dedicated car phones which are permanently installed in your car and which are obviously no use to you as a boat owner.
2 Transmobiles, which can be fitted in a vehicle but by detaching the aerial and transceiver, which takes about 30 seconds, can

be carried around. They are powered out of the vehicle by their own rechargeable battery.

3 Hand held portables. These are often called 'Yuppie' phones and are small enough to put in a pocket or briefcase.

Both transmobiles and hand held portables would have some use on a small boat.

Cellular radio

This is a system whereby phones are linked by radio rather than by lines to the telephone socket. You can therefore use them while moving around. The phone is connected by radio to the base station nearest to you. Each base station covers a particular area or 'cell'. Cells overlap so that as you move around you have continuous coverage.

Two companies operate networks. Racal Vodaphone (a subsidiary of Racal Electronics) who call their network Vodaphone, and Telecom Securicor Cellular Radio, rather a mouthful, known as Cellnet. This is a subsidiary of British Telecom. These companies can only set up the cellular radio network; they are not allowed to sell equipment or send out bills.

There are many firms who can supply phones and a browse through the adverts in Sunday newspapers will give you some idea of what's on offer. In general, a cellphone working on one network will not work through the other.

Equipment is fairly expensive to buy although prices have come down a lot in recent years; it is possible to lease phones if you are in business. In addition to the basic cost of buying or renting the phone there is a one off connection charge and a monthly line rental for the system you use. Calls are appreciably dearer than normal charges and peak and off-peak rates apply as with domestic calls.

One of the main advantages of cellular phones for the boat owner is that you can make calls without going through a Coast Station, and it is a much more private medium. However the system has not been developed specifically for boat owners, so the emphasis has been on building up the cells around major cities. Having said that, most of the country is covered by one system or the other and both are rapidly increasing their number of cells and filling in the gaps. The coverage offshore is not so easy to judge, although along the south coast of England in particular, it is almost continuous.

Equipment charges vary greatly from supplier to supplier. If you decide to rent, shop around as call charges, installation fees and even the length of charge unit can vary considerably. At first, its use was limited to businessmen and the like who had phones in their cars and who needed to be available at all times. More recently, some major shipping companies, whose ships trade around the coast, have started to fit their vessels with these phones, but to the small boat owner they remain very much in the luxury bracket.

The same limitations apply as with CB. Although it is possible to dial 999 and speak to the Coastguard none of the other rescue services can use the system. The equipment is not waterproof either. As an example of this, the telephone rang in the middle of the night at a Coast Station and at the other end was a trawler skipper using his cell phone.

'I've got a pain in my back. I want to talk to a doctor.'

He was told that he could not be connected to a doctor unless he called the station on VHF. 'That will cost me an arm and a leg,' he replied without humour, at which point he was told that Medico calls on VHF are free while the call he was presently engaged on was, in fact, costing him an arm and a leg. His reply is not printable but he eventually spoke to a doctor. . . on VHF.

Appendix A   Phonetic alphabet

Alpha	November
Bravo	Oscar
Charlie	Papa
Delta	Quebec
Echo	Romeo
Foxtrot	Sierra
Golf	Tango
Hotel	Uniform
India	Victor
Juliet	Whiskey
Kilo	Xray
Lima	Yankee
Mike	Zulu

Appendix B   Glossary of procedural words

Affirmative Correct.
All after Repeat everything after the word or phrase indicated.
All before Repeat everything before the word or phrase indicated.
All between ... and ... Repeat everything between the words or phrases indicated.
Correct You are correct.
Correction The last word or phrase was wrong. (This should be followed by **I say again.**)
FEENEE Follows **SEELONCE** or **PRUDONCE** to indicate that distress working has finished and the channel can be used as normal.

I spell I will spell the last word phonetically.

MAYDAY The international signal used on radio telephony to indicate that your vessel is in grave and imminent danger.

MAYDAY RELAY Signal made by HM Coastguard or BT Coast Station when re-broadcasting a distress message.

Nothing heard I have not heard any reply to my transmission.

Out End of conversation.

Over Invitation to the other station to transmit.

PAN PAN The signal used to prefix an urgency message.

PRUDONCE Indicates that the channel is available for use but traffic should be minimised. You should listen carefully before you speak.

Radio check Request to the other station to give the strength and readability of your signal.

Read back Repeat the message you have just received.

Roger I have received you last transmission satisfactorily.

Say again Repeat your last message.

SECURITE Pronounced SAYCUREETAY. It is used to prefix a safety message.

SEELONCE DISTRESS A command used by a station other than the one controlling the distress to impose radio silence for normal traffic during distress working.

SEELONCE FEENEE End of radio silence.

SEELONCE MAYDAY A command used by the station controlling a distress to impose radio silence for normal traffic during distress working.

Station calling (your boat's name)
The way to address a station that has called you but whose identity is in doubt. (Not to be used if you only *think* someone has called you.)

Word after (normally used with **Repeat**) A request to repeat the word after the one given.

Word before (normally used with **Repeat**) A request to repeat the word before the one given.

Appendix C Glossary of terms used in radio

Accounting authority Asked for by Coast Radio Stations to enable them to bill link calls correctly. For UK yachts it is GB14.

Callsign All vessels with a radio licence are issued a callsign which either consists of four letters or four letters and a number or a combination eg GBVC, MWGJ4. Most small craft have one of the last two.

Channel 16 The distress and calling channel.

Coast Radio Stations Radio stations situated around the coast which are operated by British Telecom. They are the only stations authorised to make ship to shore link calls. They also broadcast weather forecasts, gale and navigational warnings.

Dual watch The facility on some VHF sets which allows you to monitor two channels at the same time, usually Channel 16 and a selected channel.

Duplex The facility on a radio which allows normal two way conversation. This is only used on link calls.

FM Frequency Modulation; the technical term for the way signals are formed and transmitted on VHF.

MHz Megahertz. The frequency of radio waves in millions of cycles per second.

Private channel A VHF channel outside the international channels allocated to a particular user and not available for general use.

PTT Switch Press to Talk switch. Used in Simplex and Semi Duplex mode to switch on the transmitter. It must be released to hear the receiver.

Public correspondence channel Duplex channels used by Coast Radio Stations for link calls.

R/T Radio telephone.

Selcall Selective Calling. A system of coded signals to alert specific stations that another is calling them.

Semi Duplex Used in link calls when a full Duplex service is not possible. The craft uses its equipment in Simplex mode while the shore user can use Duplex.

Simplex A facility on a radio which allows a station to transmit and receive, but not at the same time.

Squelch A circuit in a radio which suppresses background noise.

Traffic List A list broadcast by Coast Radio Stations giving the names and callsigns of vessels for which there are link calls.

VHF Very High Frequency; the band of frequencies used by marine radio.

Working channel The channel on which business is carried out after an initial call on Channel 16.

YTD Yacht Telephone Debit; a system used by British Coast Radio Stations on VHF whereby the cost of a link call is debited to the caller's home telephone number.

Appendix D   Coastguard Maritime Rescue Centres

MRSC Shetland

MRSC Pentland

MRSC Stornoway

MRCC Aberdeen

MRSC Oban

MRSC Forth

MRCC Clyde

MRSC Tyne Tees

MRSC Belfast

MRSC Humber

MRSC Holyhead

MRSC Liverpool

MRCC Yarmouth

MRCC Swansea

MRSC Thames

MRSC Milford Haven

MRSC Portland

MRSC Solent

MRCC Dover

MRSC Brixham

MRCC Falmouth

Appendix E   BTI Coast Radio Stations

Appendix F Coast Radio Station information

The first channel given is the station's primary channel and is also used for making broadcasts. In addition Channel 64 on Lands End is used for broadcasts to vessels to the south of the Isles of Scilly.

Stations in capitals are manned stations.

Coast station	VHF channels	Broadcast group *(times of broadcast for each group are given in Appendix G)*
North Foreland	26 5 65 66	A
Hastings	7 63	A
Thames	2 83	A
Orfordness	62 82	A
HUMBER	26 24 85	A
Bacton	7 3 63 64	A
Grimsby	27 4	A
LANDS END	27 64 85 88	B
Pendennis	62 66	B

Coast station	VHF channels	Broadcast group (*see Appendix G*)
Start Point	26 60 65	B
NITON	28 4 64 81 85 87	B
Weymouth Bay	5	B
Ilfracombe	5 7	B
Burnham	25	No Broadcasts made
Celtic	24	B
Hebrides	26	C
Lewis	5	C
Skye	24	C
Oban	7	C
PORTPATRICK	27	C
Clyde	26	C
Islay	25 60	C
Morecambe Bay	4 82	C
Anglesey	26 28 61	C
Cardigan Bay	3	C
CULLERCOATS	26	D
Whitby	25 28	D
STONEHAVEN	26	D
Forth	24 62	D
Buchan	25 87	D
WICK	No VHF	
Cromarty	28 84	D
Orkney	26	D
Shetland	27	D
Collafirth	24	D

In the following areas use these specific channels:

Brighton Marina	Ch 4
Scillies	Ch 64
River Severn	Ch 7
River Mersey	Ch 28
Morecambe Bay gas field	Ch 61
The Wash	Ch 85

Appendix G   Coast Radio Station broadcast times

Broadcast group	Navigation warnings	Gale warnings	Weather forecasts
A	0133	0303	
	0533	0903	0733
	0933	1503	
	1333	2103	1933
	1733		
	2133		
B	0233	0303	
	0633	0903	0733
	1033	1503	
	1433	2103	1933
	1833		
	2233		
C	0203	0303	
	0603	0903	0703
	1003	1503	
	1403	2103	1903
	1803		
	2203		
D	0233	0303	
	0633	0903	0703
	1033	1503	
	1433	2103	1903
	1833		
	2233		

Appendix H   Useful addresses

**British Telecom
Aeronautical and Maritime
(NIA313)**
1st Floor
43 Bartholomew Close
London EC1A 7HP

**Department of Trade and
Industry
Radio Communications
Division**
Waterloo Bridge House
Waterloo Road
London SE1 8UA

Department of Transport
HM Coastguard Publicity
Unit
Room S13/11,2
Marsham St
London SW1P 3EB

Meteorological Office
MET 01
Eastern Rd
Bracknell
Berks RG12 2SZ

**Royal Yachting
Association**
RYA House
Romsey Road
Eastleigh
Hants SO5 4YA

**BT COAST RADIO
STATIONS**

BT Radio Station Dean
Whitwell Rd
Ventnor
Isle of Wight
PO38 2AB

**BT Radio Station
Dunnotar Mains Farm**
Stonehaven
Kincardineshire
AB3 2TL

**BT Radio Station
Portpatrick**
Stranraer
DG9 8TG

BT Radio Station
Skewjack
St. Levan
Penzance TR19 6NB

BT Radio Station
Trusthorpe
Mablethorpe
Lincolnshire LN12 2PH

BT Radio Station
Whitley Bay
Tyne & Wear NE26 2PD

BT Radio Station Wick
Caithness
KW1 5LT

COASTGUARD
MARITIME RESCUE
CENTRES AND THEIR
ASSOCIATED SUB
CENTRES

MRCC ABERDEEN
Marine House
Blaikies Quay
Aberdeen AB1 2PB
Tel: 0224 592334

MRSC Shetland
The Knab
Knab Road
Lerwick
Shetland ZE1 0AX
Tel: 0579 2976

MRSC Pentland
Cromwell Rd
Kirkwall
Orkney KW15 1LN
Tel: 0856 3268

MRSC Forth
Fifeness
Crail
Fife KY10 3XN
Tel: 0333 50666

MRCC YARMOUTH
Haven Bridge House
Great Yarmouth NR30 1HZ
Tel: 0493 851338

MRSC Tyne Tees
Priory Grounds
Tynemouth
Tyne & Wear NE30 4DA
Tel: 091 2572691

MRSC Humber
Limekiln Lane
Bridlington
North Humberside YO15 2LX
Tel: 0262 672317

MRCC DOVER
Langdon Battery
Swingate
Dover CT15 5NA
Tel: 0304 210008

MRSC Thames
East Terrace
Walton-on-Naze
Essex CO14 8PY
Tel: 0255 675518

MRCC FALMOUTH
Pendennis Point
Castle Drive
Falmouth
Cornwall TR11 4WZ
Tel: 0326 317575

MRSC Solent
Whytecroft House
44A Marine Parade West
Lee-on-Solent
Hants PO13 9WR
Tel: 0705 552100

MRSC Portland
Custom House Quay
Weymouth
Dorset DT4 8BE
Tel: 0305 760439

MRSC Brixham
Kings Quay
Brixham
Devon TQ5 9TW
Tel: 0803 882704

MRCC SWANSEA
Tutt Head
Mumbles
Swansea SA3 4ZL
Tel: 0792 366534

MRSC Milford Haven
St Annes Head
Dale
Haverfordwest
Dyfed SA62 3RD
Tel: 0646 636218

MRSC Holyhead
Newry Beach Road
Holyhead
Anglesey
Gwynedd LL65 1ET
Tel: 0407 762051

MRSC Liverpool
Hall Road West
Crosby
Liverpool L23 8SY
Tel: 051 931 3341

MRCC CLYDE
Navy Buildings
Eldon St
Greenock PA16 7QY
Tel: 0475 29988

MRSC Belfast
Orlock Head
Groomsport
Bangor
Co. Down BT19 2LH
Tel: 0247 883184

MRSC Oban
Boswell House
Argyll Square
Oban PA34 4BD
Tel: 0631 63720

MRSC Stornoway
4 South Beach
Stornoway
Isle of Lewis PA87 2LH
Tel: 0851 2013

Index